DAILY PRAYER
WITH MOTHER TERESA

Daily Prayer
With Mother Teresa

PRAYERS AND MEDITATIONS FOR
EVERY DAY OF THE YEAR

COMPILED BY
Brother Angelo Devananda

Fount

An Imprint of HarperCollins*Publishers*

Fount Paperbacks is an Imprint of
HarperCollins*Religious*
Part of HarperCollins*Publishers*
77–85 Fulham Palace Road,
Hammersmith, London W6 8JB

First published in the United States of America by
Servant Books, Ann Arbor, Michigan in 1986 and
in Great Britain by Fount Paperbacks, London in 1987
under the title *Jesus the Word To Be Spoken*

This edition published in Great Britain in 1994
by Fount Paperbacks
3 5 7 9 10 8 6 4

A catalogue record for this book is
available from the British Library

ISBN 0 00 627835 3

Printed and bound in Great Britain by
HarperCollinsManufacturing Glasgow

Dedication

To my parents: Pasquale Scolozzi and Candida
   Marotta.
To my siblings: Franco, Lucio, and Rosalba.
To my brothers the unlovable, the dejected, the unworthy, all the
   spiritually poorest,
   under whose distress Jesus is disguised
   as "Eucharist of compassion" to feed hunger; and
to the countless young people of the new generations,
   anxious about their life:
that *Jesus the Word to Be Spoken* be an open invitation to
them to come and see, so that they may choose to go
and serve.

Acknowledgment

My heartfelt thanks to Henry Dieterich for selecting and processing the quotations from Mother Teresa and helping me in all kinds of ways to put this book together against winds and tides.

Know the Word, love the Word, live the Word, give the Word. Mary, first carrier of God's Word, help the Universal Brothers of the Word to become humble like you, so that they can become holy like Jesus. God bless you.
—Mother Teresa, M.C.

Introduction

IN THE MINDS OF MANY PEOPLE, Mother Teresa of Calcutta evokes strong and striking associations with the world of hunger and poverty. At the time of the famine in Biafra, the image of the little nun in a white sari bordered in blue, clutching a dying child to her bosom, caught the attention of the world. Truly in my mind and heart Mother's image is one of nurturing. Her total life is dedicated to quenching Christ's thirst for souls; she is truly fed by this hunger and thirst.

Almost ten years ago I joined the "Society," as Mother Teresa's religious family of the Missionaries of Charity is called. At my first meeting with Mother, she explained to me a vision for a contemplative brotherhood geared to evangelize the poor, and she asked for my cooperation: "Jesus has made himself Eucharistic food to satiate our human hunger; in response we should feed him in the distressing disguise of the poorest through the Word of life." The only difference between the Brothers of the Word and the Missionaries of Charity Sisters, she said, would be that for them faith in action was service and for us faith in action would be contemplation. "It is easy to remove the physical need for food, for clothing, for shelter; it is difficult to respond to that terrible loneliness, that terrible hurt in the heart."

Again in her Nobel Prize acceptance speech in 1979, she said that the poverty of the West is much more difficult to remove: "When I pick up a person from the streets hungry, I give him a plate of rice, a piece of bread, and I have satisfied that hunger; but a person that is shut out, that feels unwanted, unloved, terrified, the person that has been thrown out of society—how much more difficult it is to remove that hunger."

This indeed echoes Christ's teaching in the gospel, that not by bread alone does man live, but by every word that proceeds from the mouth of God.

In 1976, the creation in the Bronx of a contemplative branch of the Missionaries of Charity Sisters was Mother Teresa's direct response to the theme of the Philadelphia Eucharistic Congress: "Hunger for God."

One year later the Brothers of the Word were founded. Echoing the rule of the Sisters, this is how she described the purpose of the brotherhood:

"Our aim is to quench the thirst of Jesus on the Cross for love of souls and the hunger of souls for him, Word and Bread of Life."

Mother Teresa has never fallen victim to the illusion that she can end poverty in the world, much as she would like to do so. She has always told me that our work is but a drop in the ocean; yet she seems satisfied to add, "The world is more aware of people dying of starvation in the street. This cannot be ignored any more." At the core of poverty there always seems to be fear, as in the story of an agonized child that Mother tells: "A few weeks ago, I picked up a child from the street, and from the face I could see that little child was hungry. I didn't know, I couldn't make out how many days that little one had not eaten. So I gave her a piece of bread, and the little one took the bread and, crumb by crumb, started eating it. I said to her, 'Eat, eat the bread. You are hungry.' And the little one looked at me and said, 'I am afraid. When the bread will be finished, I will be hungry again.'"

For us in the West, poverty and fear are of a different kind: that there will not be enough for us to accept one more life, to feed one more mouth, to educate one more child, to share one more place. To make a searching and fearless moral inventory of ourselves, the courage to change the things in us that we can change, is the remedy of our sickness. Let us not forget that spiritual poverty, particularly in our society, is the result of greed, dishonesty, and pride.

Jesus presents poverty in the Gospels as blessedness; true poverty, real detachment, frees and at the same time enriches us. It is a gift of grace and a mystical call to the possession of the kingdom within.

When I joined Mother Teresa in the adventure of beginning a new brotherhood to bring Jesus the Word to the spiritually poor, I discovered to my great surprise that my journey toward the poverty of the poorest turned out to be an agonizing journey into my own spiritual poverty. I would not have survived without the particular grace of understanding that the interior pain that transforms us is a special gift of God's love.

At a particularly hurtful time at the beginning of our brotherhood, when I felt entirely at a loss, Mother wrote: "Don't be afraid. There must be the cross, there must be suffering—a clear sign that Jesus has drawn you so close to his heart that he can share his suffering with you."

Indeed there is a very austere, ascetical element in Mother's way of life and teaching, yet the secret of "loving until it hurts" is the key to the paradox of blessedness in the world of poverty.

Pope John Paul II, a great friend of Mother Teresa, used an impressive image during his visit to Haiti when he spoke of the missionaries and their life. To convey their great willingness to serve, aided by only a few tools or none at all, he simply said they are "working with naked hands."

When I first came to Haiti to work for the evangelization of the slum dwellers in Saint Martin sans Fil, I was overwhelmed by an intense feeling of powerlessness, only overcome later by a total surrender, by which I came to know that truly Jesus is master of the impossible. In the words of my favorite passage from our rule: "With Jesus our Savior, lamb led to the slaughter, and with the poor, we will accept cheerfully and in a spirit of faith all the opportunities he gives us of a greater gift: to share in the silence, loneliness, and agony of his Passion in our own life, due to humiliations, misunderstanding, false blame, rejections, failures, incapacities, corrections, temptations, lack of virtue, separation, sickness, old age, and death."

Mother's teachings are like the treasure hidden in the field of which the gospel tells, full of simplicity, personal experience, and common sense. Words of wisdom prompted by the need to form her Sisters or the Brothers reflect her own younger days in formation as a Sister of Our Lady of Loreto and the experience and intuitive knowledge gained as she has survived with integrity of spirit the many hard and painful situations of her own life.

Mother was a high school teacher before founding

the Missionaries of Charity. That pedagogical element is still in her; she will repeat the same concept again and again with tireless persistence. This characteristic appears in the present collection of daily quotations from Mother.

Before her reception of the Nobel Peace Prize in 1979, Mother Teresa belonged mainly to us, her children, and to the poor in the institutions she founded. Since then, she has become a world figure, holding ambassadorial status from the Vatican, like a true missionary of charity, a universal mother figure, and ambassador of God's love to the poorest everywhere. With tireless courage, she is always going in haste, frequently attempting the impossible. Often where others have had to leave or have failed for political reasons, war, or persecution, she has been invited in.

From her initial inspiration in 1946 to the present, the Missionaries of Charity Sisters have grown to be over 3000 individuals working in 313 houses in 75 different countries of the world.

In 1963, a male branch, known as the Missionaries of Charity Brothers, was added by Mother, with the cooperation of Brother Andrew, a priest from Australia.

The International Association of Co-Workers was approved by Pope Paul VI in 1969 and affiliated to the Society of the Missionaries of Charity.

The contemplative sisters in New York, founded in 1976, were called for a short time Sisters of the Word, and are now simply Missionaries of Charity Contemplative.

In 1977, she started the Universal Brothers of the

Word. Recently two more male branches have been added to the Missionaries of Charity family: the Missionaries of Charity Brothers Contemplative in Rome, and the Missionaries of Charity Fathers in New York.

Our brotherhood, the Universal Brothers of the Word, is canonically separate from the Missionaries of Charity, although we fully share in the common spiritual inheritance of Mother Teresa. We retain our initial identity of the Word, as an inspiration of Mother herself, and are directly spiritually connected to her. Externally we differ from the rest of her family in three main ways: We run no particular institutions for the proclamation of the Word; we limit our work of evangelization to part of the day; and we support ourselves by the work of our hands. Our constitutions are a faithful reflection of those of the Sisters, with more emphasis on the contemplative element, and respond to our specific call for the Word.

This book presents 366 "words of wisdom," one for each day of the year, drawn from Mother's instructions, anecdotes, and meditations, arranged with some correspondence to the major religious themes of the year. Limitations of time and material have prevented me from preparing a more compact and logical volume; my personal desire has been to respond to the spiritual need of my Brothers and to feed them with Mother's inspiration, teaching, and examples. I hope that persons in all walks of life may benefit from this collection, spending a bit of each day with Mother Teresa. Mindful of the imperfections of this volume, let me conclude in Mother's own way:

To Jesus be the glory and to me be the blame!

Mary, first carrier of the Word, pray for us.

—Brother Angelo Devananda

First Month

1 It is difficult to pray if you don't know how to pray, but we must help ourselves to pray. The first means to use is silence. Souls of prayer are souls of great silence. We cannot put ourselves directly in the presence of God if we do not practice internal and external silence. Therefore we shall take as a special point silence of mind, eyes, and tongue.

2 Silence of the tongue will teach us so much: to speak to Christ, to be joyful at recreation, and to have many things to say. At recreation Christ speaks to us through others and at meditation he speaks to us directly. Silence also makes us so much more Christlike because he had a special love for this virtue.

3 Then we have the silence of the eyes which will always help us to see God. Our eyes are like two windows through which Christ or the world comes to our hearts. Often we need great courage to keep them closed. How often we say, "I wish I had not seen this thing," and yet we take so little trouble to overcome the desire to see everything.

4 The silence of the mind and of the heart: our Lady "kept all these things in her heart." This silence brought her close to our Lord, so that she never had to regret anything. See what she did when St. Joseph was troubled. One word from her would have cleared his mind; she did not say that word, and our Lord himself worked the miracle to clear her name. Would that we could be so convinced of this necessity of silence! I think then the road to close union with God will become very clear.

5 Silence gives us a new outlook on everything. We need silence to be able to touch souls. The essential thing is not what we say but what God says to us and through us. Jesus is always waiting for us in silence. In that silence, he will listen to us, there he will speak to our soul, and there we will hear his voice.

6 The interior silence is very difficult, but we must make the effort to pray. In silence we will find new energy and true unity. The energy of God will be ours to do all things well, and so will the unity of our thoughts with his thoughts, the unity of our prayers with his prayers, the unity of our actions with his actions, of our life with his life. All our words will be useless unless they come from within. Words which do not give the light of Christ increase the darkness.

7 This will need much sacrifice, but if we really mean to pray and want to pray we must be ready to do it now. These are only the first steps towards prayer but if we never make the first step with determination, we will not reach the last one: the presence of God.

8 Prayer, to be fruitful, must come from the heart and must be able to touch the heart of God. See how Jesus taught his disciples to pray. Call God your Father; praise and glorify his name. Do his will as the saints do it in heaven; ask for daily bread, spiritual and temporal; ask for forgiveness of your own sins and that you may forgive others, and also for the grace not to give in to temptations and for the final grace to be delivered from the evil that is in us and around us.

9 The apostles asked Jesus to teach them to pray, and he taught them the beautiful prayer, the Our Father. I believe each time we say the Our Father, God looks at his hands, where he has carved us—"I have carved you on the palm of my hand"—he looks at his hands, and he sees us there. How wonderful the tenderness and love of the great God!

10 We should be professionals in prayer. The apostles understood this very well. When they saw that they might be lost in a multitude of works, they decided to give themselves to continual prayer and to the ministry of the word. We have to pray on behalf of those who do not pray.

11 Pray lovingly like children, with an earnest desire to love much and to make loved the one that is not loved.

12 We must be aware of our oneness with Christ, as he was aware of oneness with his Father. Our work is truly apostolic only in so far as we permit him to work in us and through us, with his power, with his desire, and with his love.

13 In reality, there is only one true prayer, only one substantial prayer: Christ himself. There is only one voice which rises above the face of the earth: the voice of Christ. The voice reunites and coordinates in itself all the voices raised in prayer.

14 Perfect prayer does not consist in many words but in the fervor of the desire which raised the heart to Jesus. Jesus has chosen us to be souls of prayer. The value of our actions corresponds exactly to the value of the prayer we make, and our actions are fruitful only if they are the true expression of earnest prayer. We must fix our gaze on Jesus, and if we work together with Jesus we will do much better. We get anxious and restless because we try to work alone, without Jesus.

15 Often our prayers do not produce results because we have not fixed our mind and heart on Christ, through whom our prayers can ascend to God. Often a deep fervent look at Christ may make the most fervent prayer. "I look at him and he looks at me" is the most perfect prayer.

16 "A family that prays together stays together," said Fr. Peyton about the family rosary. How much more should this apply to us! Living together, working together, praying together is an aid to piety, a safeguard to chastity, and a mutual advantage in the work for souls. We should not get into the habit of postponing our prayers but make them with the community.

17 He taught us to learn from him, to be meek and humble of heart. If we are meek and humble, we will love each other as he loves us. That is why we should ask again and again that we bring prayer back into our families. The family that prays together stays together. And to stay together you will love one another as God loves you, and he loves you tenderly.

18 Unity is the fruit of prayer, of humility, of love. Therefore, if the community prays together, it will stay together, and if you stay together you will love one another as Jesus loves each one of you. A real change of heart will make it really one heart full of love. This one heart our community offers to Jesus and to our Lady, his mother.

19 Failure and loss of vocation also come from neglect of prayer. As prayer is the food of spiritual life, neglect of prayer starves the spiritual life and loss of vocation is unavoidable. Let us ask our Lady in our own simple way to teach us how to pray, as she taught Jesus in all the years that he was with her in Nazareth.

20 There are many who do not know, many who do not dare, and many who do not want to pray. In the communion of saints we act and pray in their names.

21 Love to pray, feel the need to pray often during the day, and take the trouble to pray. If you want to pray better, you must pray more. Prayer enlarges the heart until it is capable of containing God's gift of himself. Ask and seek, and your heart will grow big enough to receive him and keep him as your own.

22 We want so much to pray properly and then we fail. We get discouraged and give up on prayer. God allowed the failure but he did not want the discouragement. He wants us to be more childlike, more humble, more grateful in prayer, and not to try to pray alone, as we all belong to the mystical body of Christ, which is praying always. There is always prayer; there is no such thing as "I pray," but Jesus in me and Jesus with me prays; therefore the body of Christ prays.

23 "I kept the Lord ever before my eyes, because he is ever at my right hand that I may not slip," says the psalmist. God is within me, a more intimate presence than that whereby I am in myself: "In him we live and move and have our being." It is he who gives life to all, who gives power and being to all that exists. But for his sustaining presence, all things would cease to be and fall back into nothingness. Consider that you are in God, surrounded and encompassed by God, swimming in God.

24 Jesus Christ has told us that we ought "always to pray and not to faint," that is, not to grow weary of doing so. St. Paul says, "Pray without ceasing." God calls all men to this disposition of the heart, of praying always. Let the love of God once take entire and absolute possession of a heart; let it become to that heart like a second nature; let that heart suffer nothing that is contrary to it to enter; let it apply itself continually to increase this love of God by seeking to please him in all things and refusing him nothing that he asks; let it accept as from his hand everything that happens to it; let it have a firm determination never to commit any fault deliberately and knowingly; or if it should fall, to be humble for it and to rise up again at once. Such a heart will pray continually.

25 To pray generously is not enough; we must pray devoutly, with fervor and piety. We must pray perseveringly and with great love.

26 The knowledge we impart must be Jesus crucified, and as St. Augustine says: "Before allowing his tongue to speak, the apostle ought to raise his thirsting soul to God and then give forth what he has drunk in, and pour forth what he has been filled with"; or as St. Thomas tells us: "Those who are called to the works of the active life would be wrong in thinking that their duty dispenses them from the contemplative life. This duty adds to it and does not lessen its necessity."

27. These two lives, action and contemplation, instead of excluding each other, call for each other's help, implement and complete each other. Action, to be productive, has need of contemplation. The latter, when it gets to a certain degree of intensity, diffuses some of its excess on the first. By contemplation the soul draws directly from the heart of God the graces which the active life must distribute.

28 For us religious, prayer is a sacred duty and sublime mission. Conscious of the many urgent needs and interests we carry in our hands, we will ascend the altar of prayer, take up our rosary, turn to all the other spiritual exercises with great longing, and go with confidence to the throne of grace, that we may obtain mercy and find grace and seasonable aid for ourselves and our souls.

29 Our prayers are mostly vocal prayers; they should be burning words coming forth from the furnace of a heart filled with love. In these prayers, speak to God with great reverence and confidence. Pray with folded hands, downcast eyes, and lifted hearts, and your prayers will become like a pure sacrifice offered unto God. Do not drag or run ahead; do not shout or keep silent but devoutly, with great sweetness, with natural simplicity, without any affectation, offer your praise to God with the whole of your heart and soul. We must know the meaning of the prayers we say and feel the sweetness of each word to make these prayers of great profit; we must sometimes meditate on them and often during the day find our rest in them.

30 The prayer that comes from the mind and heart and which we do not read in books is called mental prayer. We must never forget that we are bound by our state to tend toward perfection and to aim ceaselessly at it. The practice of daily mental prayer is necessary to reach our goal. Because it is the breath of life to our soul, holiness is impossible without it. St. Teresa of Avila says, "She who gives up mental prayer does not require the devil to push her into hell; she goes there of her own accord." It is only by mental prayer and spiritual reading that we can cultivate the gift of prayer. Mental prayer is greatly fostered by simplicity, that is forgetfulness of self, by mortifications of the body and of our senses, and by frequent aspirations which feed our prayer. "In mental prayer," says St. John Vianney, "shut your eyes, shut your mouth, and open your heart." In vocal prayer we speak to God, in mental prayer he speaks to us. It is then that God pours himself into us.

31 The best means for making spiritual progress is prayer and spiritual reading. *Tolle et lege,* (take and read) St. Augustine was told, and after reading his whole life was changed. So too was that of St. Ignatius, the wounded soldier, when he read the lives of the saints. How often we ourselves have found the light pouring into our souls during spiritual reading. St. Thomas à Kempis writes, "Take then a book into thy hands as Simeon the just man took the child Jesus into his arms; and when you have finished, close the book and give thanks for every word out of the mouth of God, because in the Lord's field you have found a hidden treasure." St. Bernard says, "Try not so much to catch the meaning as to relish what you read. Let us not die of starvation in the midst of abundance." There is indeed little advantage in reading if we do not read well. Spiritual reading is one of the most precious spiritual exercises and duties, one that no one can afford to neglect. When choosing a book, never take something above you, but always take one which will give you the greatest spiritual profit.

Second Month

1 Confession makes the soul strong because a really good confession—the confession of a child in sin coming back to her Father—always begets humility, and humility is strength. We may go to confession as often as we want and to whom we want, but we are not encouraged to seek spiritual direction from any and every source. The confessional is not a place for useless conversation or gossip. The topic should be my sins, my sorrow, my forgiveness: how to overcome my temptations, how to practice virtue, how to increase in the love of God.

2 First, confession; after it ask for spiritual direction if necessary. The reality of my sins must come first. For most of us there is the danger of forgetting that we are sinners and must go to confession as sinners. We must want the precious blood to wash away our sins.

We must go to God to tell him we are sorry for all we have done which may have hurt him.

3 One thing is necessary for us—confession. Confession is nothing but humility in action. We called it penance, but really it is a sacrament of love, a sacrament of forgiveness. That is why confession should not be a place in which to talk for long hours about our difficulties. It is a place where I allow Jesus to take away from me everything that divides, that destroys. When there is a gap between me and Christ, when my love is divided, anything can come to fill the gap. We should be very simple and childlike in confession. "Here I am as a child going to her Father." If a child is not yet spoiled and has not learned to tell lies, he will tell everything. This is what I mean by being childlike. Confession is a beautiful act of great love. Only in confession can we go as sinners with sin and come out as sinners without sin.

4 You need only ask at night before you go to bed, "What did I do to Jesus today? What did I do for Jesus today? What did I do with Jesus today?" You have only to look at your hands. This is the best examination of conscience.

5 And how will you find Jesus? He has made it so easy for us. "Love one another as I loved you." If we have gone astray, we have the beautiful sacrament of confession. We go to confession a sinner full of sin. We come from confession a sinner without sin by the greatness of the mercy of God. No need for us to despair. No need for us to commit suicide. No need

for us to be discouraged—no need, if we have understood the tenderness of God's love. You are precious to him. He loves you, and he loves you so tenderly that he has carved you on the palm of his hand. These are God's words written in the Scripture. You know that. Remember that when your heart feels restless, when your heart feels hurt, when your heart feels like breaking—then remember, "I am precious to him. He loves me. He has called me by my name. I am his. He loves me. God loves me." And to prove that love he died on the cross.

6 One evening a gentleman came to our house and told me, "There is a Hindu family with eight children, and they have not eaten for a long time. Do something for them." I took some rice, and I went straightaway. I could see in the children's faces terrible hunger. And yet when the mother took the rice she divided it in two portions and went out. When she came back I asked her, "Where did you go? What did you do?" She gave me one answer only: "They are hungry also." She had next-door neighbors, a Muslim family, and she knew they were hungry. I did not bring any more rice for that day because I wanted them to experience the joy of giving. I was not surprised that she gave, but I was surprised that she knew that they were hungry. Do we know? Do we have time to know? Do we have time even to smile at somebody?

7 The poor are very wonderful people. One evening we went out and picked up four people from the street. One of them was in a most terrible condition. I told the sisters, "You take care of the other three; I will take care of this one that looks worse." So I did for her all that my love can do. I put her in bed, and there was such a beautiful smile on her face. She took hold of my hand, as she said one word only: "thank you"— and she died.

8 I never forgot the opportunity I had in visiting a home where they had all these old parents of sons and daughters who had just put them in an institution and forgotten them. I went there, and I saw in that home they had everything, beautiful things, but everybody was looking toward the door. And I did not see a single one with a smile on their face. And I turned to the Sister and I said, "How is that? How is it that these people who have everything here, why are they all looking toward the door? Why are they not smiling?"

I am so used to seeing smiles on our people; even the dying ones smile. She said, "This happens nearly every day. They are expecting, they are hoping that a son or a daughter will come to visit them." They are hurt because they are forgotten. And see—this is where love comes. That poverty comes right into our own home, even neglect of love. Maybe in our own family we have somebody who is feeling lonely, who is feeling sick, who is feeling worried, and these are difficult days for everybody. Are we there? Are we there to receive them?

9 The poor people are very great people. They can teach us so many beautiful things. The other day one of them came to thank us and said, "You people who have vowed chastity, you are the best people to teach us family planning because it is nothing more than self-control out of love for each other." And I think he said something beautiful. These are people who maybe have nothing to eat, but they are great people.

10 Our children, we want them, we love them; but what of the other millions? Many people are very, very concerned with the children of India, with the children of Africa, where quite a number die of malnutrition, of hunger, and so on. But millions of others are dying by the will of their own mothers. And this is what is the greatest destroyer of peace today. Because if a mother can kill her own child, what is left before I kill you and you kill me? There is nothing in between.

11 I was surprised in the West to see so many young boys and girls given to drugs, and I tried to find out why. Why is it like that? And the answer was, "Because there is no one in the family to receive them." Father and mother are so busy they have no time. The child goes back out on the street and gets involved in something. We are talking of peace. These are things that break peace.

12 One day I was walking down the streets of London. I saw a man, huddled up, looking so lonely, looking so alone. Then he asked me to bend down, so I stopped, took his hand, shook his hand, asked him how he was. My hand is always very warm, and he looked up and said, "Oh, after such a long time, I feel the warmth of a human hand after such a long time." And his eyes brightened up, and he sat up. Just that little warmth of a human hand brought joy into his life. You have to experience that. You must have your eyes wide open and do it.

13 In Australia, where our Sisters are working, we go to the houses of the poor and wash and clean and do all kinds of things there. Then I went to one man's house, and I asked him, "May I clean your house?" And he said, "I'm all right." I said, "You'll be more all right if you let me do it." So he allowed me to clean his place. And then I saw in the corner of his room a big lamp full of dirt. I asked him, "Don't you light this lamp?" He said, "For whom? For years nobody has come to me—for years." So I said, "Will you light the lamp if the Sisters come?" He said, "Yes." So I cleaned the lamp. The Sisters started going to his house, to his place, and the lamp was lit. I completely forgot about him. After two years I got news from him saying, "Tell my friend the light she has lit in my life is still burning."

14 The more repugnant the work, the greater should be our faith and cheerful devotion. That we feel the repugnance is but natural, but when we overcome it for love of Jesus we may become heroic. Very often it has happened in the lives of the saints that a heroic overcoming of something repugnant has been the key to a high sanctity. Such was the case of St. Francis of Assisi, who when meeting a leper completely disfigured, drew back, but then overcoming himself, kissed the terrible disfigured face. The result was that Francis was filled with an untold joy.

He became the complete master of himself and the leper walked away praising God for his cure.

15 When we handle the sick and the needy we touch the suffering body of Christ and this touch will make us heroic; it will make us forget the repugnance and the natural tendencies in us. We need the eyes of deep faith to see Christ in the broken body and dirty clothes under which the most beautiful one among the sons of men hides. We shall need the hands of Christ to touch these bodies wounded by pain and suffering.

16 A Sister was telling me that just two or three weeks ago she and some other Sisters picked up a man from the streets in Bombay and brought him home. We have a big place donated to us which we have turned into a home for the dying. This man was brought there and the Sisters took care of him. They loved him and treated him with dignity. Right away they discovered that the whole of his back had no skin, no flesh. It was all eaten up. After they washed him they put him on his bed, and this Sister told me that she had never seen so much joy as she saw on the face of that man. Then I asked her, "What did you feel when you were removing those worms from his body; what did you feel?" And she looked at me and said, "I've never felt the presence of Christ; I've never really believed the word of Jesus saying, 'I was sick and you did it to me.' But his presence was there and I could see it on that man's face." This is the gift of God.

17 As you know, we have got our Brothers also who are Missionaries of Charity. One of our Brothers loves the lepers. We are taking care of 49,000 lepers in India. This Brother really loves the lepers. He came one day after he had had some difficulties with his superior. He said to me, "I love the lepers; I want to be with them. I want to work for them. My vocation is to be with the lepers." I said to him, "Brother, you are making a mistake. Your vocation is not to work for the lepers. Your vocation is to belong to Jesus. The work for the lepers is only your love for Christ in action; and, therefore, it makes no difference to anyone as long as you are doing it to him, as long as you are doing it with him. That's all that matters. That is the completion of your vocation, of your belonging to Christ."

18 We are the servants of the poor. We give wholehearted, free service to the poor. In the world the people are paid for their work. We are paid by God. We are bound by a vow to love and serve the poor, and to live as the poor with the poor.

19 Do we treat the poor as our dustbins to give whatever we cannot use or eat? I cannot eat this food so I will give it to the poor. I cannot use this thing or that piece of cloth so I will give it to the poor. Am I then sharing the poverty of the poor? Do I *identify* myself with the poor I serve? Am I one with them? Do I share with them as Jesus shared with me?

20 A few weeks ago two young people came to our house, and they gave me lots of money to feed the people. I said to them, "Where did you get so much money?" They said, "Two days ago we got married. Before our wedding we decided: we will not buy wedding clothes, we will not have a wedding feast, we will give you the money." I know what that means for a Hindu family, and how big a sacrifice they had made. Then I asked them, "But why did you do it?" And they said, "We love each other so much that we wanted to share the joy of loving with the people you serve. And we experienced the joy of loving." And where does this love begin?—at home. And how does it begin?—by sharing until it hurts, by loving until it hurts.

21 We cook for 9,000 people every day. One day one Sister came and said, "Mother, there's nothing to eat, nothing to give to the people." I had no answer. And then by 9:00 that morning a truck full of bread came to our house. The government gives a slice of bread and milk to the poor children. That day—no one in the city knew why—but suddenly all the schools were closed. And all the bread came to Mother Teresa. See, God closed the schools. He would not let our people go without food. And this was the first time, I think, in their lives that they had had such good bread and so much. This way you can see the tenderness of God.

22 One day in Calcutta a man came with a prescription and said, "My only child is dying and this medicine can be brought only from outside of India." Just at that time, while we were still talking, a man came with a basket of medicine. Right on the top of that basket, there was this medicine. If it had been inside, I would not have seen it. If he had come before, or if he had come afterward, I could not have seen it. But just at that time, out of the millions and millions of children in the world, God in his tenderness was concerned with this little child of the slums of Calcutta enough to send, just at that time, that amount of medicine to save that child. I praise the tenderness and the love of God, because every little one, in a poor family or a rich family, is a child of God, created by the Creator of all things.

23 We need to avoid pride. Pride destroys everything. That's why Jesus told his disciples to be meek and humble. He didn't say contemplation is a big thing—but being meek and humble with one another. If you understand that, you understand your vocation. To live his way is the key to being meek and humble.

24 If you are put in the kitchen, you must not think it does not require brains—that sitting, standing, coming, going, anything will do. God will not ask that Sister how many books she has read; how many miracles she has worked; but he will ask her if she has done her best, for the love of him. Can she in all sincerity say, "I have done my best"? Even if the best is a failure, it must be our best, our utmost.

25 Let none glory in their success but refer all to God in deepest thankfulness; on the other hand, no failure should dishearten them as long as they have done their best. Humanly speaking, if a Sister fails in her work we are inclined to attribute it to all kinds of human weaknesses—she has no brains, she did not do her best, and so on. Yet in the eyes of God she is not a failure if it is her best. She is his co-worker still.

26 We must never think anyone of us is indispensable. God has ways and means—he may allow everything to go upside-down in the hands of a talented and capable Sister. God sees only her love. You may be exhausted with work, even kill yourself, but unless your work is interwoven with love it is useless. God does not need our work.

27 It may happen that children repeatedly fail in their religious examination when being prepared for First Communion. Do not give in to discouragement. No more must you do so when you try to save a marriage or convert a sinner and you do not succeed. If you are discouraged it is a sign of pride because it shows you trust in your own powers. Never bother about people's opinions. Be humble and you will never be disturbed.

28 Today, when everything is being questioned and changed, let us go back to Nazareth. Jesus had come to redeem the world, to teach us the love of his Father. How strange that he should spend thirty years just doing nothing, wasting his time! Not giving a chance to his personality or to his gifts! We know that at the age of twelve he silenced the learned priests of the Temple, who knew so much and so well. But when his parents found him, he went down to Nazareth and was subject to them. For twenty years we hear no more of him, so that the people were astonished when he went in public to preach. He, a carpenter's son, doing just the humble work in a carpenter's shop for thirty years!

29 Humility is nothing but truth. "What have we got that we have not received?" asks St. Paul. If I have received everything, what good have I of my own? If we are convinced of this we will never raise our head in pride. If you are humble, nothing will touch you, neither praise nor disgrace, because you know what you are. If you are blamed you will not be discouraged, if they call you a saint you will not put yourself on a pedestal. If you are a saint, thank God. If you are a sinner, do not remain so.

Third Month

1 The contemplative and apostolic fruitfulness of our way of life depends on our being rooted in Christ Jesus our Lord by our deliberate choice of small and simple means for the fulfillment of our mission and by our fidelity to humble work of love among the spiritually poorest, identifying ourselves with them, sharing their poverty and insecurities until it hurts.

2 We need to be pure in heart to see Jesus in the person of the spiritually poorest. Therefore the more disfigured the image of God is in that person, the greater will be our faith and devotion in seeking Jesus' face and lovingly ministering to him. We consider it an honor to serve Christ in the distressing disguise of the spiritually poorest; we do it with deep gratitude and reverence in a spirit of fraternal sharing.

3 We the Universal Brothers of the Word run no permanent institutions for the proclamation of the word of God. However, we avail ourselves of every opportunity we can to proclaim his redeeming love, wherever we can find the spiritually poorest. Part of each day will be spent in the proclamation of the good news. We will deal not with crowds but with individuals, person to person, family to family, or, when necessary, with small groups where close contact is possible.

4 Like Jesus, who submitted himself to the common law of labor and the common lot of the poor, we the Universal Brothers of the Word will labor hard in any work assigned to us and rejoice to have the opportunity to do humble work. If there is no other means available, the brothers will support themselves by the work of their hands, either in the cultivation of the land, in craftsmanship, or in some other appropriate self-employment in accordance with our way of life, avoiding, however, engaging in any money-making business.

5 In his Passion our Lord says, "Thy will be done. Do with me what you want." And that was the hardest thing for our Lord even at the last moment. They say that the Passion in Gethsemane was much greater than even the crucifixion. Because it was his heart, his soul that was being crucified, while on the cross it was his body that was crucified. That's why on the cross he never said, "Thy will be done." He accepted in silence, and he gave his mother, and he said, "I thirst" and "It is finished." But nowhere, not once did he say, "Thy will be done" because he had already totally accepted the Father's will during that terrible struggle of the isolation and the loneliness. And the only way that we know that it was so difficult for him at that hour is that he asked, "Why could you not spend one hour with me?"—we know he needed consolation. This is total surrender: not to be loved by anybody, not to be wanted by anybody, just to be a nobody because we have given all to Christ.

6 St. Therese, the Little Flower, explained surrender very beautifully when she said, "I am like a little ball in the hand of Jesus. He plays with me. He throws me away, puts me in the corner. And then like a little child who wants to see what is inside, he tears the ball apart and throws the pieces away." This is what a brother, a sister, has to be, that little ball in the hand of Jesus, who says to Jesus, "You can do whatever you want, as you want, when you want, as long as you want."

7 We are at his disposal. If he wants you to be sick in bed, if he wants you to proclaim his word in the street, if he wants you to clean the toilets all day, that's all right, everything is all right. We must say, "I belong to you. You can do whatever you like." And this, Brothers, is our strength and this is the joy of the Lord.

8 Right from the very beginning, learn to obey. It will lead you straight to God. You don't have to ride this crooked life. There is a very straight way to the heart of Jesus. You will never, never go astray, never make a mistake, if you understand the difference. The superior who tells you to do this or do that may make a mistake. I may make a mistake and tell the Sisters do this and go here and go there. But that Sister who does what I tell her is infallible. So it is for you Brothers. This conviction is total surrender.

9 What Jesus did when he became man was his total surrender to his Father. Again and again we hear the word "Father." As he was preaching, when he was teaching, when he was with the people, continually he taught the word "Father." "I have come to do the will of my Father." "I have been sent by the Father." "My Father and I are one." "I love you as the Father loves me." All the time the Father is in his words. He belongs so much to the Father that there is no separation, no division. There was no doubt. There was no question at all. And this is what a Universal Brother of the Word has to be: complete oneness with Christ, complete oneness with the word of God. And that word of God, that joy that you receive in prayer and adoration and contemplation, in that aloneness with God, that same word you are to give to others.

10 Our vocation is to belong to Jesus. The easiest way and the simplest way of belonging is this: the Holy Spirit makes us do that giving of self, that total surrender to God, without any reflection, without any counting the cost. We call that "blind surrender." It is like our Lady: when she knew that the Lord was calling, she said yes. And she never withdrew that yes. It was a blind, continual yes in her life. It is the same thing for us. The whole of our life must come to that one word yes. Yes to God: that is holiness. We allow God to take from us whatever he wants and we accept whatever he gives with joy. That is yes in action.

11 We must know exactly when we say yes to God what is in that yes. Yes means "I surrender," totally, fully, without any counting the cost, without any examination, "Is it all right? Is it convenient?" Our yes to God is without any reservations. That's what it is to be a contemplative. I belong to him so totally that there are no reservations. It doesn't matter what we feel.

12 The word of God becomes flesh during the day, during meditation, during Holy Communion, during contemplation, during adoration, during silence. That word in you, you give to others. It is necessary that the word live in you, that you understand the word, that you love the word, that you live the word. You will not be able to live that word unless you give it to others.

13 Total surrender to God must come in small details just as it comes in big details. It's nothing but that single word, "Yes, I accept whatever you give, and I give whatever you take." And this is just a simple way for us to be holy. We must not create difficulties in our own minds. To be holy doesn't mean to do extraordinary things, to understand big things, but it is a simple acceptance, because I have given myself to God, because I belong to him—my total surrender. He could put me here. He could put me there. He can use me. He cannot use me. It doesn't matter because I belong so totally to him that he can do just what he wants to do with me.

14 Lent is a time when we relive the Passion of Christ. Let it not be just a time when our feelings are roused, but let it be a change that comes through cooperation with God's grace in real sacrifices of self. Sacrifice, to be real, must cost; it must hurt; it must empty us of self. Let us go through the Passion of Christ day by day.

15 During Lent we shall in a special way and with deep feeling meditate on the Passion of our Lord and examine our conscience on what sin of ours caused that special pain to Jesus. I will make reparation and share that pain by doubling my penance. I shall keep strict custody of my eyes; I shall keep clean thoughts in my mind; I shall touch the sick with greater gentleness and compassion; I shall keep the silence of the heart with greater care, so that in the silence of my heart I hear his words of comfort, and from the fullness of my heart I comfort Jesus in the distressing disguise of the poor. I shall confess especially my neglect of penance.

16 We often pray, "Let me share with you your pain; I want to be the spouse of Jesus crucified," and yet when a little spittle of an uncharitable remark or a thorn of thoughtlessness is given to us, how we forget that this is the time to share with him his shame and pain.

17 During this Lent let us improve our spirit of prayer and recollection. Let us free our minds from all that is not Jesus. If you find it difficult to pray, ask him again and again, "Jesus, come into my heart, pray in me and with me, that I may learn from thee how to pray." If you pray more you will pray better. Take the help of all your senses to pray.

18 The first step to becoming holy is to will it. St. Thomas says, "Sanctity consists in nothing else than a firm resolve, the heroic act of a soul abandoning herself to God. By an upright will we love God, we choose God, we run toward God, we reach him, we possess him." O good, good will which transforms me into the image of God and makes me like him!

19 To resolve to be a saint costs much. Renunciations, temptations, struggles, persecutions, and all kinds of sacrifices surround the resolute soul. One can love God only at one's own expense.

20 Penance is absolutely necessary for us. Nothing is of greater force in restraining the disordered passions of the soul and in subjecting the natural appetites to right reason. Then we shall possess those heavenly joys and delights that surpass the pleasure of earth as much as the soul does the body, and heaven the earth.

21 As Jesus can no longer live his Passion in his body, Mother Church gives the opportunity to allow Jesus to live his Passion and death in our body, heart, and soul. Even so, there is no comparison with his Passion. Still we need so much grace just to accept whatever he gives and give whatever he takes with joy, love, and a smile.

22 In his Passion Jesus taught us how to forgive out of love, how to forget out of humility. So let us at the beginning of the Passion of Christ examine our hearts fully and see if there is any unforgiven hurt or unforgotten bitterness.

23 Let us often say during the day, "Wash away my sins and cleanse me from all my iniquity." How it must hurt Jesus dwelling in our heart to feel in our hearts this bitterness, this hurt, this revengeful feeling made of jealousy and pride! My children, let us be sincere and ask to be forgiven. Is my love for the other members of the community so great, so real as to forgive, not out of duty but out of love?

24 We are but instruments that God deigns to use; these instruments bring forth fruit in the measure that they are united to God, as St. Paul says: "I have planted, Apollos watered, but God gave the increase." We obtain grace in proportion to our sanctity, to our fervor, and to our degree of union with our Lord. Sanctity is the soul of the true apostolate. Therefore, we must apply ourselves heart and soul to the learning of this sanctity.

25 A day alone with Jesus is apt to spur us on in the vigorous pursuit of holiness through personal love for Jesus. Jesus desires our perfection with unspeakable ardor. "For this is the will of God, your sanctification." His Sacred Heart is filled with an insatiable longing to see us advance towards holiness.

26 You must allow the Father to be a gardener, to prune. You will be pruned, don't worry. He has his own way of pruning you. You must allow him to do it. Take the people in the novitiate at Tor Fiscale, for example. They have really pruned the vine there. I was looking at it and I wondered, "How can leaves or branches or fruit come on this thing?" But a man who knows vines well pruned it, and he has pruned it right up to the ends of the stems. How branches will come, how leaves will come, how the fruit will come, I don't know. But quite possibly if I come here after two months I will see it all hung with grapes because of all the pruning. It is the same for you. Now you have been pruned well, cut off completely, and you don't see anything—no leaves, no branches, nothing.

27 Suffering has to come because if you look at the cross, he has got his head bending down—he wants to kiss you—and he has both hands open wide— he wants to embrace you. He has his heart opened wide to receive you. Then when you feel miserable inside, look at the cross and you will know what is happening. Suffering, pain, sorrow, humiliation, feelings of loneliness, are nothing but the kiss of Jesus, a sign that you have come so close that he can kiss you.

28 Do you understand, Brothers? Suffering, pain, humiliation—this is the kiss of Jesus. At times you come so close to Jesus on the cross that he can kiss you. I once told this to a lady who was suffering very much. She answered, "Tell Jesus not to kiss me—to stop kissing me." That suffering has to come that came in the life of our Lady, that came in the life of Jesus—it has to come in our life also. Only never put on a long face. Suffering is a gift from God. It is between you and Jesus alone.

29 To be able to love Christ with undivided love and chastity through the freedom of poverty, in the total surrender of obedience and wholehearted free service to the poorest of the poor and others as Christ loves you and me while we await his coming in glory: this is the whole rule of life of the Universal Brothers of the Word. Let Jesus use you without consulting you, and you will be holy because you belong to him.

30 Our total surrender will come today by surrendering even our sins so that we will be poor. "Unless you become a child you cannot come to me." You are too big, too heavy; you cannot be lifted up. We need humility to acknowledge our sin. The knowledge of our sin helps us to rise. "I will get up and go to my Father."

31 It must have been so hard to have been scourged, to have been spat upon. "Take it away," Jesus prayed during his agony. His Father didn't come to him directly and say, "This is my be-

loved Son," but he consoled him through an angel.
Let us pray that we will fill our hearts with Jesus'
surrender, that we will understand total surrender.

Fourth Month

1 If day after day we devote ourselves to the perfect fulfillment of our spiritual duties, he will gradually admit us to a closer intimacy so that even outside the time dedicated to prayer we shall find no difficulty in remaining conscious of the divine presence. On the other hand, the diligent practice of the presence of God by means of fervent aspirations in our labors and in our recreations will be rewarded with more abundant graces. We must endeavor to live alone with Jesus in the sanctuary of our inmost heart.

2 If we earnestly desire holiness, self-denial must enter our lives fully after prayer. The easiest form of self-denial is control over our bodily senses. We must practice interior mortification and bodily penances also. How generous are we with God in our mortifications?

3 The aim of taking a retreat is to advance in the knowledge and love of God, to purify ourselves, and to reform and transform our lives according to the life of our model, Jesus Christ. It is a time of greater silence, of more fervent prayer, of special penance, and more intense spiritual activity. It is not so much a looking back on the achievements and failure of the past, as a looking forward to a more generous imitation of our Lord himself.

4 I fulfill what is wanting in the Passion of Christ. It is very difficult to understand what the connection is between our penances and the Passion of Christ. We must constantly follow in the footsteps of Jesus Christ and in a certain manner crucify our own flesh. Our suffering will never come to that degree reached by the saints and martyrs.

5 Remember that the Passion of Christ ends always in the joy of the resurrection of Christ, so when you feel in your own heart the suffering of Christ, remember the resurrection has to come, the joy of Easter has to dawn. Never let anything so fill you with sorrow as to make you forget the joy of Christ risen.

6 May the joy of the risen Jesus Christ be with you, to bring joy into your very soul. The good God has given himself to us. "Joy" said the angel in Bethlehem. In his life, Jesus wanted to share his joy with his apostles, "That my joy may be in you." Joy was the password of the first Christians. St. Paul—how often he repeats himself: "Rejoice in the Lord always, again I say to you, rejoice." In return for the great grace of baptism, the priest tells the newly baptized, "May you serve the church joyfully."

7 Easter is one of the feasts of our Society, a feast of joy—the joy of the Lord. Let nothing so disturb us, so fill us with sorrow or discouragement, as to make us forfeit the joy of the resurrection.

8 May the joy of our risen Lord be your strength in your work, your way to the Father, your light to guide you and your bread of life.

9 May the joy and love of the risen Jesus be always with you, in you, and among you, so that we all become the true witnesses of his Father's love for the world: "For God loved the world so much that he gave his Son." Let us also love God so much that we give ourselves to him in each other and in his poor.

10 Jesus has chosen us for himself; we belong to him. Let us be so convinced of this belonging that we do not allow anything, however small, to separate us from this belonging—from this love.

11 What is dependence on divine providence? A firm and lively faith that God can and will help us. That he can is evident because he is almighty. That he will is certain because he promises it in so many passages of Scripture and because he is infinitely faithful to all his promises. Christ encourages us to this lively confidence in these words: "Therefore I tell you, whatever you ask in prayer, believe that you have received it, and it will be yours" (Mk 11:24).

Therefore the apostle Peter also commands us to throw all cares upon the Lord who provides for us. And why should God not care for us since he sent us his Son and with him all? St. Augustine says: "How can you doubt that God will give you good things since he vouchsafed to assume evil for you?"

12 This must excite in us confidence in the providence of God who preserves even the birds and the flowers. Surely if God feeds the young ravens which cry to him, if he nourishes the birds which neither sow nor reap nor gather into barns, if he vests the flowers of the field so beautifully, how much more will he care for men whom he has made in his own image and likeness and adopted as his children, if we only act as such, keep his commandments, and always entertain a filial confidence in Him.

13 Knowledge will make you strong as death. Love Jesus generously. Love him trustfully, without looking back and without fear. Give yourself fully to Jesus—he will use you to accomplish great things on the condition that you believe much more in his love than in your weakness. Believe in him— trust in him with blind and absolute confidence because he is Jesus. Believe that Jesus and Jesus alone is life—and sanctity is nothing but that same Jesus intimately living in you; then his hand will be free with you. Give yourself unswervingly, conforming yourself in all things to his holy will which is made known to you through your superior.

14 Love Jesus with a big heart. Serve Jesus with joy and gladness of spirit, casting aside and forgetting all that troubles and worries you. To be able to do all these, pray lovingly like children, with an earnest desire to love much and make loved the love that is not loved.

15 Trust in the good God who loves us, who cares for us, who sees all, knows all, can do all things for my good and the good of souls. One thing Jesus asks of me: that I lean upon him; that in him alone I put complete trust; that I surrender myself to him unreservedly. I need to give up my own desires in the work of my perfection. Even when all goes wrong, and I feel as if I were a ship without a compass, I must give myself completely to him.

16 I must not attempt to control God's actions; I must not count the stages in the journey he would have me make. I must not desire a clear perception of my advance along the road, nor know precisely where I am on the way of holiness. I ask him to make a saint of me, yet I must leave to him the choice of that saintliness itself and still more the choice of the means which lead to it.

17 Am I convinced of Christ's love for me and mine for him? This conviction is like sunlight which makes the sap of life rise and the buds of sanctity bloom. This conviction is the rock on which sanctity is built. What must we do to get this conviction? We must know Jesus, love Jesus, serve Jesus. We know him through prayers, meditations, and spiritual duties. We love him through holy Mass and the sacraments and through that intimate union of love.

18 What is our spiritual life? A love union with Jesus, in which the divine and the human give themselves completely to one another. All that Jesus asks of me is to give myself to him in all poverty and nothingness.

19 "I will be a saint" means I will despoil myself of all that is not God. I will strip my heart and empty it of all created things; I will live in poverty and detachment. I will renounce my will, my inclinations, my whims and fancies, and make myself a willing slave to the will of God. Yes, my children, this is what I pray for daily—for each one—that we each may become a slave to the will of God.

20 The church of God needs saints today. This imposes a great responsibility on us Sisters, to fight against our own ego and love of comfort that leads us to choose a comfortable and insignificant mediocrity. We are called upon to make our lives a rivalry with Christ; we are called upon to be warriors in a sari, for the church needs fighters today. Our war cry has to be "Fight—not flight."

21 We ought every day to renew our resolution and to rouse ourselves to fervor, as if it were the first day of our conversion, saying, "Help me, Lord God, in my good resolve and in thy holy service, and give me grace this very day really and truly to begin, for what I have done till now is nothing." This is the spirit in which we should begin our monthly recollection day.

22 Our ideal is no one but Jesus. We must think as he thinks, love as he loves, wish as he wishes; we must permit him to use us to the full. It is beautiful to see the humility of Christ—"Who being in the form of God did not think it robbery to be equal with God, but emptied himself, taking the form of a servant, being made in the likeness of men and in habit found as man."

23 The humility of Jesus can be seen in the crib, in the exile in Egypt, in the hidden life, in the inability to make people understand him, in the desertion of his apostles, in the hatred of his persecutors, in all the terrible suffering and death of his Passion, and now in his permanent state of humility in the tabernacle, where he has reduced himself to such a small particle of bread that the priest can hold him with two fingers. The more we empty ourselves, the more room we give God to fill us.

24 Let there be no pride nor vanity in the work. The work is God's work; the poor are God's poor. Work for Jesus and Jesus will work with you, pray with Jesus and Jesus will pray through you. The more you forget yourself, the more Jesus will think of you. The more you detach yourself from self, the more attached Jesus is to you. Put yourself completely under the influence of Jesus so that he may think his thoughts in your mind, do his work through your hands—for you will be all-powerful with him who strengthens you.

25 The church wants "renewal." Renewal does not mean changing a habit and a few prayers. Renewal is faithfulness to the spirit of the constitutions, a spirit which seeks holiness by means of a poor and humble life, the exercise of sincere and patient charity, spontaneous sacrifice and generosity of heart, and which finds its expression in purity and candor.

26 In our meditations we should always ask Jesus, "Make me a saint according to your own heart, meek and humble." "Learn of me," he insisted. We must say it in the spirit in which he meant it. We know him better now through our gospel lessons and meditations, but have we understood him in his humility? Does his humility appeal to us? Attract us?

27 Our knowledge of self must be clear—of the good in us as well as the bad. Each one of us has plenty of good as well as plenty of bad inside.

28 "The kingdom of heaven is like a merchant seeking precious pearls." Yes, we have promised great things but greater things are promised us. Be faithful to Christ and pray for perseverance. Remember to say to yourself, "I have been created for greater things." Never stoop lower than the ideal. Let nothing satisfy you but God.

29 Let us thank God for all his love for us, in so many ways and in so many places. Let us in return, as an act of gratitude and adoration, determine to be holy because he is holy. Each time Jesus wanted to prove his love for us, he was rejected by mankind. Before his birth, his parents asked for a simple dwelling place and there was none.

30 In each of our lives Jesus comes as the bread of life—to be eaten, to be consumed by us. This is how he loves us. Then Jesus comes in our human life as the hungry one, the other, hoping to be fed with the bread of our life, our hearts by loving, and our hands by serving. In loving and serving, we prove that we have been created in the likeness of God, for God is love and when we love we are like God. This is what Jesus meant when he said, "Be perfect as your Father in heaven is perfect."

Fifth Month

1 It is very, very important for us to have a deep love for our Lady. For she was the one who taught Jesus how to walk, how to pray, how to wash, how to do all the little things that make our human life so beautiful. She had to do them. And the same thing now—she will always be willing to help us and teach us how to be all for Jesus alone, how to love only Jesus, how to touch him and see him, to serve him in the distressing disguise.

2 Mary was a true missionary because she was not afraid to be the handmaid of the Lord. She went in haste to put her beautiful humility into a living action of love, to do the handmaid's work for Elizabeth. We know what this humility obtained for the unborn child: he "leapt with joy" in the womb of his mother—the first human being to recognize the coming of Christ; and then the mother of the Lord sang with joy, with gratitude, and praise.

3 The greatness of our Lady was in her humility. No wonder Jesus, who lived so close to her, seemed to be so anxious that we learn from him and from her but one lesson: to be meek and humble of heart.

4 No one has learned so well the lesson of humility as Mary did. She, being the handmaid of the Lord, was completely empty of self, and God filled her with grace. "Full of grace" means full of God. A handmaid is at someone's disposal, to be used according to someone's wish with full trust and joy, to belong to someone without reserve. This is one main reason for the spirit of the Society.

Total surrender: to be at God's disposal, to be used as it pleases, him to be his handmaid, to belong to him.

5 She will teach us her humility: though full of grace—yet only the handmaid of the Lord; though the mother of God—yet serving like a handmaid in the house of Elizabeth; though conceived Immaculate—she meets Jesus humiliated, carrying his cross, and near the cross she stands as one of us, as if she were a sinner needing redemption.

Like her, the greater are the graces we have received, let us with greater and more delicate love touch the lepers, the dying, the lonely, the unwanted.

Like her, let us always accept the cross in whatever way it may come.

Humility of the heart of Mary, fill my heart. Teach me as you taught Jesus to be meek and humble of heart and so glorify our Father.

6 Let us beg from our Lady to make our hearts "meek and humble" like her Son's was. It was from her and in her that the heart of Jesus was formed.

7 How much we can learn from our Lady! She was so humble because she was all for God. She was full of grace. She made use of the almighty power that was in her: the grace of God.

8 See how our Lady obeyed the angel: "Be it done to me according to thy word. "Whose word? The angel's—because he took the place of God. He was sent by God to her. She, the queen of heaven, obeys the angel. See how she obeyed St. Joseph, with what love and submission, without an excuse. To her, St. Joseph was "He" whose place he took.

9 Our Lady was full of God because she lived for God alone, yet she thought of herself only as the handmaid of the Lord. Let us do the same.

10 We read in the Gospel that God loved the world so much that he gave his Son. He gave him to an ordinary, simple, young woman. She was the most pure, the most holy human being. And she on receiving him—knowing who he was—just said, "Humble me. Be done to me according to thy word." What was the word? "Be the mother of Jesus." And that's why I always say, no one in the world could have been a better priest than Mary the most pure. Yet she remained only the handmaid of the Lord. Jesus did not consecrate her.

11 During this time of grace let us, in a special way, ask our Lady to teach us her silence, her kindness, her humility.

Silence of Mary speak to me, teach me how with you and like you I can learn to keep all things in my heart as you did, not to answer back when accused or corrected, to pray always in the silence of my heart as you did.

12 Let us ask our Lady to be with us. Let us ask her to give us her heart so beautiful, so pure, so immaculate—her heart so full of love and humility that we may be able to receive Jesus as the bread of life, that we may love him as she loved him and serve him in the distressing disguise of the poor.

13 We have all tried in some way or another to be a real joy to our Lady. So often during the day, we call her the "cause of our joy" because the joy of her Son is our strength. Let us promise that we will make our community another Bethlehem, another Nazareth. Let us love each other as we love Jesus. In Nazareth there was love, unity, prayer, sacrifice, and hard work; and there was especially a deep understanding and appreciation of each other and thoughtfulness for each other.

14 We need a very deep life of prayer to be able to love as he loves each one of us. We must ask our Lady, "Dear mother, teach me to love, prepare me." It's not enough just to join a priesthood or a brotherhood or sisterhood. That's not enough. We need to be more and more humble like Mary and holy like Jesus. If only we are humble like Mary, we can be holy like Jesus. That's all: holy like the Lord.

15 Because God loves the world he sent his Son. Now he sends you to be his word, and that word has to take flesh in the hearts of the people. That's why you need our Lady; when the word of God came to her, became flesh in her, then she gave it to others. It is the same for you. The word of God has come to you and has become flesh in you and then you must be able to give that love.

16 Mary in the mystery of her annunciation and visitation is the very model of the way you should live, because first she received Jesus in her life, then she went in haste to give to her cousin Elizabeth; what she had received, she had to give. You must be like her, giving in haste the word you have received in meditation. In every Holy Communion, Jesus the word becomes flesh in our life, a special, delicate, beautiful gift of God; it's a privilege—why you, the Brothers of the Word, and not someone else, I don't know. But you must protect it with tender care because he is giving himself, the Word, to you to be made flesh, to each one of you, and to those who will come after.

17 Jesus wants us to be holy as his Father is. We can become very great saints if we only want to. Holiness is not the luxury of the few, but a simple duty for you and for me.

18 While we are preparing for the coming of the Holy Spirit, I pray for you that the Holy Spirit may fill you with his purity, so that you can see the face of God in each other and in the faces of the poor you serve. I ask the Holy Spirit to free you of all impurity—body, soul, mind, will, and heart—that each one of you become the living tabernacle of God Most High, and so become a carrier of God's love and compassion. Ask the Holy Spirit to make you a sinner without sin.

19 We shall make this year one of peace in a particular way. To be able to do this we shall try to talk more to God and with God and less with men and to men. Let us preach the peace of Christ as he did. He went about doing good; he did not stop his works of charity because the Pharisees and others hated him or tried to spoil his Father's work. He just went about doing good. Cardinal Newman wrote, "Help me to spread Thy fragrance everywhere I go; let me preach thee without preaching, not by words but by my example."

20 Our lives, to be fruitful, must be full of Christ; to be able to bring his peace, joy, and love we must have it ourselves, for we cannot give what we have not got—the blind leading the blind. The poor in the slums are without Jesus and we have the privilege of entering their homes. What they think of us does not matter, but what we are to them does matter. To go to the slums merely for the sake of going will not be enough to draw them to Jesus. If you are preoccupied with yourself and your own affairs, you will not be able to live up to this ideal.

21 If you give to the people a broken Christ, a lame Christ, a crooked Christ, deformed by you, that is all they will have. If you want them to love him, they must know him first. Therefore, give the whole Christ first to the Sisters, then to the people in the slums: Christ full of zeal, love, joy, and sunshine. Do I come up to the mark? Am I a dark light, a false light, a bulb without the connection, having no current, therefore shedding no radiance? Put your heart into being a bright light. Say to Christ, "Help me to shed thy fragrance everywhere I go." Our very name explains this rule. Sisters of the slums, carriers of Christ's love.

22 In the slums the Sisters should find a place where they will gather the little street children, whoever they may be. Their first concern is to make them clean, feed them, and only then teach them, just a little reading and writing. Religion must be proposed to them in a simple, interesting, and attractive way. Whatever the Sisters teach, first there must always be something the children can enjoy and yet at the same time learn.

23 Let the Sisters bring the children to Mass. Do your best to get them. If you have to run for a child, do it and God in his infinite mercy may give the light and grace to that soul because of all the trouble you took. Never lose sight of the mercy of God. Take the trouble to help the children to love the Mass, to know the meaning of the Mass, to join in the Mass through simple prayers and hymns. Be careful of the attitude you take while minding the children during Mass. Do not correct loudly. Keep your hands joined.

Join in the prayers and the singing. The children will do exactly what you do.

24 In their visits let the Sisters encourage true devotion to the Sacred Heart and the family rosary. They should induce the Catholic families to be consecrated to the Sacred Heart and to the Immaculate Heart of Mary. We have to try our utmost to keep the families together, remembering that "the family that prays together stays together." There are so many broken homes—the wife here, the husband there. Teach them that happiness can't be found without prayer. Even in old age there is no security against temptation.

25 All over the world, there is terrible suffering, terrible hunger for love. So bring prayer in your family, bring it to your little children. Teach them to pray. For a child that prays is a happy child. A family that prays is a united family. We hear of so many broken families. And then we examine them: why are they broken? I think because they never pray together. They are never one in prayer before the Lord.

26 When visiting the families you will meet with very much misery. Sometimes you will find a little child watching near a dying parent, or holding the head of a dead parent. It is then that you must put out all your energy to help that little child in his sorrow. Once there were found two little children near the dead body of their father, who had died two days before. Thank God, Sisters came and rescued the children and arranged a proper burial for the father.

27 Our bishop has approved of our baptizing the dying. Nirmal Hriday is only a means. If it were only a matter of washing and cleaning, it would be closed today. But for the opportunities it affords to reach souls, it is most important. In Nirmal Hriday we understand better the value of a soul.

28 Sometime back, I picked up this man off the street, covered with dirt and worms. He was eaten up alive. The only part of his body that was clean was his face. There were crawling worms on his body. I took him to our home. And he said then, "I have lived like an animal in the street. I am going to die like an angel, loved and cared for." It took us three hours to clean him, to remove everything from his body. And then he said, "Sister, I am going home to God." And he died. He really went home to God with such a beautiful smile on his face. I've never seen a smile like that. There was this man who had lived like an animal in the streets, eaten up alive by worms. And yet, he had courage. And he was looking forward. There was peace and joy in his face because somebody loved him, somebody wanted him, somebody helped him to die in peace with God.

29 Recently, one great Brazilian man, a man of high position, wrote to me that he had lost faith in God and man. He gave up his position and everything and only wanted to commit suicide. One day, as he was passing by a shop, his eyes suddenly fell on a TV in the window. There was the scene of Nirmal Hriday, the Sisters looking after the sick and dying. He wrote to me that after seeing that scene, he knelt and prayed for the first time in many years. Now he has decided to turn back to God and have faith in humanity because he saw that God still loves the world.

30 The very fact that God has placed a certain soul in your way is a sign that God wants to do something for her. It is not chance—it has been planned by God. We are bound in conscience to help. If a soul desires God, she has the right to be given the means to go to him. No one has the right to stand between. Look at the cross and you will know what one soul means to Jesus.

31 Zeal for souls is the effect and the proof of true love of God. We cannot but be consumed with the desire for saving souls, the greatest and dearest interest of Jesus. Therefore, zeal is the test of love and the test of zeal is devotedness to his cause—spending life and energy in the work of souls.

Sixth Month

1 "Thou shalt love the Lord thy God with thy whole heart, with thy whole soul, and with all thy mind." This is the command of our great God, and he cannot command the impossible. Love is a fruit, in season at all times and within the reach of every hand. Anyone may gather it and no limit is set. Everyone can reach this love through meditation, the spirit of prayer, and sacrifices, by an intense interior life. Do I really live this life?

2 I want you all to fill your hearts with great love. Don't imagine that love, to be true and burning, must be extraordinary. No; what we need in our love is the continuous desire to love the One we love.

3 To possess God we must allow him to possess our souls. How poor we would be if God had not given us the power of giving ourselves to him; how rich we are now! How easy it is to conquer God! If we give ourselves to him, then God is ours, and there can be nothing more ours than God. The money with which God repays our surrender is himself. We become worthy of possessing him when we abandon ourselves completely to him.

4 Total surrender consists in giving ourselves completely to God. We must give ourselves fully to God because God has given himself to us. If God owes nothing to us and is ready to impart to us no less than himself, shall we answer with just a fraction of ourselves? Should we not rather give ourselves fully to God as a means of receiving God himself? I for God and God for me. I live for God and give up my own self, and in this way God lives for me.

5 To surrender means to offer him my free will, my reason, my own life in pure faith. My soul may be in darkness. Trial and suffering are the surest test of my blind surrender.

6 Surrender is also true love. The more we surrender, the more we love God and souls. If we really love souls, we must be ready to take their place, to take their sins upon us and expiate them in us by penance and continual mortification. We must be living holocausts, for the souls need us as such.

7 There is no limit to God's love. It is without measure and its depth cannot be sounded. This is shown by his living and dying among us. Now turn the same picture around. There must be no limit to the love that prompts us to give ourselves to God, to be the victim of his unwanted love, that is, the love of God that has not been accepted by men.

8 Love has a hem to her garment
That reaches the very dust.
It sweeps the stains
From the streets and lanes,
And because it can, it must.

The Missionary of Charity, in order to be true to her name, must be full of charity in her own soul and spread that same charity to the souls of others, Christians and pagans.

9 Today let us recall the love of God for you and for me. His love is so tender. His love is so great, so real, so living that Jesus came just to teach us that— how to love. Love is not something that fossilizes, but something that lives. Works of love, and declaring love, is the way to peace. And where does this love begin?— right in our hearts. We must know that we have been created for greater things, not just to be a number in the world, not just to go for diplomas and degrees, this work and that work. We have been created in order to love and to be loved.

10 Again and again we hear that sentence, "Unless you become like a little child, you cannot enter into heaven." And what is being a little child? It is having a clean heart, a pure heart, a heart that holds Jesus, a heart that can say again and again, "Jesus in my heart, I believe in your tender love for me. I love you." This is the heart that you, and I, even the youngest must have to be able to look up, to look up at the cross and understand how much Jesus loved me, loved each one of us separately.

11 Our holy faith is nothing but a gospel of love, revealing to us God's love for men and claiming in return man's love for God. "God is love": a missionary must be a missionary of love. We must spread God's love on earth if we want to make souls repent wholeheartedly for sin, to strengthen them in temptation, and to increase their generosity and their desire to suffer for Christ. Let us act as Christ's love among men, remembering the words of the Imitation, "Love feels no burden, values no labors, would willingly do more than it can, complains not of impossibilities, because it conceives that it may and can do all things; when weary is not tired; when strained is not constrained; when frightened is not disturbed; but like a living flame and torch all on fire, it mounts upwards and securely passes through all opposition."

12 In our work we may often be caught in idle conversations or gossip. Let us be well on our guard, for we may be caught while visiting families. We may talk about the private affairs of this or that one and so forget the real aim of our visit. We come to bring the peace of Christ, and what if we are a cause of trouble? How our Lord will be hurt by such conduct! We must never allow people to speak against priests, religious, or their neighbors.

13 If we find that a family is in a bad mood and is sure to start a tale of uncharitableness, let us say a fervent prayer for them and then say a few things which may help them to think a little about God; then let us leave the place at once. We can do no good until their restless nerves are at peace. We must follow the same conduct with those who want to talk with the aim of wasting our precious time.

14 Love begins at home. Everything depends on how we love each other. Make your community live in this love and spread the fragrance of Jesus' love everywhere you go. Do not be afraid to love until it hurts, for this is how Jesus loved.

15 Be kind and loving with each other, for you cannot love Christ in his distressing disguise if you cannot love Jesus in the heart of your Brothers and Sisters. Love, to be living, must be fed on sacrifice. Be generous with the penances and all the sacrifices that come from our poverty, and you will be able in all sincerity to say, "My God and my all."

16 The more I go around, the better I understand how very necessary it is for us to pray the work, to make the work our love for God in action. To be able to do that, how necessary it is to live that life of total surrender to God, loving trust in our superior and in each other, and cheerfulness with the poor.

17 It is not possible to engage in the direct apostolate without being a soul of prayer, without a conscious awareness and submission to the divine will.

18 We must become holy not because we want to feel holy, but because Christ must be able to live his life fully in us. We are to be all love, all faith, all purity for the sake of the poor we serve. Once we have learned to seek first God and his will, our contacts with the poor will become the means of great sanctity to ourselves and to others. Holiness is union with God; so in prayer and action alike we come from God in Christ and go to God through Christ.

19 One day St. Margaret Mary asked Jesus, "Lord, what wilt thou have me to do?". "Give me a free hand," Jesus answered. He will perform the divine work of sanctity, not you, and he asks only for your docility. Let him empty and amend you, and afterwards fill the chalice of your heart to the brim, that you in your turn may give of your abundance. See him in the tabernacle; fix your eyes on him who is the light; bring your hearts close to his divine Heart; ask him to grant you the grace of knowing him, the love of loving him, the courage to serve him. Seek him fervently.

20 From the beginning of time the human heart has felt the need to offer God a sacrifice, but as St. Paul says, "It was impossible for sins to be taken away by the blood of bulls and goats." Therefore, Jesus Christ had to offer another sacrifice, that of himself: Jesus dying on the cross is our sacrifice. Let us not think that the holy Mass is only a memorial. No, it is the same sacrifice as that which he offered on the cross. It is very consoling that this sacrifice is our sacrifice.

21 Try to increase your love for the holy Mass and the Passion of Christ by accepting with joy all the little sacrifices that come daily. Do not pass by the small gifts, for they are very precious for yourself and for others.

22 Knowledge of Christ and him in his poor will lead us to personal love. This love only can become our light and joy in cheerful service of each other. Do not forget we need each other. Our lives would be empty without each other. How can we love God and his poor if we do not love each other with whom we live and break the bread of life daily?

23 How tenderly Jesus speaks when he gives himself to his own in Holy Communion. "My flesh is meat indeed and my blood is drink indeed. He that eats my flesh and drinks my blood abides in me and I in him." Oh, what could my Jesus do more than give me his flesh for my food? No, not even God could do more nor show a greater love for me.

24 Holy Communion, as the word itself implies, is the intimate union of Jesus and our soul and body. If we want to have life and have it more abundantly, we must live on the flesh of our Lord. The saints understood so well that they could spend hours in preparation and still more in thanksgiving. This needs no explanation, for who could explain "the depth of the riches of the wisdom and knowledge of God"? "How incomprehensible are his judgments!" cried St. Paul, "And how unsearchable his ways, for who has known the mind of the Lord?"

25 When communicating with Christ in your heart after partaking of the Living Bread, remember what our Lady must have felt when the Holy Spirit overpowered her, and she who was full of grace became full with the body of Christ. The spirit in her was so strong that immediately she "rose in haste" to go and serve.

26 In the Scripture we read of the tenderness of God for the world, and we read that God loved the world so much that he gave his Son Jesus to come to be like us and to bring us the good news that God is love, that God loves you and loves me. God wants us to love each other as he loves each one of us. We all know, when we look at the cross, how Jesus loved us. When we look at the Eucharist we know how he loves us now. That's why he made himself the bread of life to satisfy our hunger for his love, and then, as if this was not enough for him, he made himself the hungry one, the naked one, the homeless one, so that you and I can satisfy his hunger for our human love. For we have been created for that. We have been created to love and to be loved.

27 Where will you get the joy of loving?—in the Eucharist, Holy Communion. Jesus has made himself the bread of life to give us life. Night and day, he is there. If you really want to grow in love, come back to the Eucharist, come back to that adoration. In our congregation, we used to have adoration once a week for one hour, and then in 1973, we decided to have adoration one hour every day. We have much work to do. Our homes for the sick and dying destitute are full everywhere. And from the time we started having adoration every day, our love for Jesus became more intimate, our love for each other more understanding, our love for the poor more compassionate, and we have double the number of vocations. God has blessed us with many wonderful vocations.

28 Look at the tabernacle—see how much this love means now. Do I know that? Is my heart so clean that I can see Jesus there? And to make it easy for you and for me to see Jesus, he made himself the bread of life, so that we can receive life, so that we may have a life of peace, a life of joy. Find Jesus, and you will find peace.

29 Every moment of prayer, especially before our Lord in the tabernacle, is a sure positive gain. The time we spend in having our daily audience with God is the most precious part of the whole day.

30 To become holy we need humility and prayer. Jesus taught us how to pray, and he also told us to learn from him to be meek and humble of heart. Neither of these can we do unless we know what is silence. Both humility and prayer grow from an ear, mind, and tongue that have lived in silence with God, for in the silence of the heart God speaks.

Seventh Month

1 Our vocation is to belong to Jesus, to belong with a conviction, not because my vocation is to work with the poor or to be a contemplative, but because I am called to belong to him in the conviction that nothing can separate me from his love. This is what will make you contemplative Brothers, that belonging with that conviction, and the fruit of that belonging will be your vow of chastity, the freedom of your poverty, the total surrender in obedience, and, especially for you Universal Brothers of the Word, that whole-hearted free service of the Word for the spiritually poorest of the poor.

2 All the religious congregations—nuns, priests, even the Holy Father— all have the same vocation: to belong to Jesus. "I have chosen you to be mine." That's our vocation. Our means, how we spend our time, may be different. Our love for Jesus in action is only the means, just like clothes. I wear this, you wear that: it's a means. But vocation is not a means. Vocation, for a Christian, is Jesus.

3 Our active Brothers and Sisters put their service into action, and contemplative Brothers and Sisters put that loving action into prayer, into penance, into adoration, into contemplation, and into the proclamation of the word that they have meditated and adored. Active and contemplative are not two different lives; it is only that one is faith in action through service, the other faith in action through prayer.

4 Faith in action through prayer, faith in action through service: each is the same thing, the same love, the same compassion. We both have to proclaim that faith, both the Sisters and the Brothers. This is something that should encourage us and should be a strength for us, that we complete each other more fully. Because we are human beings, we need this distinction, this separation, these different names. The soul, the mind, and the heart, however, have the same thing: total surrender to God. At the moment we realize that we have really done that, then we are at his disposal, and there are no more differences.

5 In the Spirit, both congregations are carriers of God's love. We the Sisters carry God's love in action, you Brothers of the Word carry God's love in evangelization, but we are both carriers, we both are missionaries. The mission of proclaiming Christ, through action or through words, is one mission, the mission of love and compassion. For the sake of making things simpler you have different names, but this is just for external reasons. Actually it is the same thing: we both work for the proclamation of God's kingdom.

6 Right from the beginning, Brothers, take the trouble to listen to the voice of God in prayer, in adoration, and in contemplation. You may go out into the street and have nothing to say—all right, but maybe there is a man standing there on the corner and you go to him. Maybe he resents you, but you are there, and that presence is there. You must radiate that presence that is within you, in the way you address that man with love and respect. Why? Because you believe that is Jesus. Jesus cannot receive you: for this you must know how to go to him. He comes disguised in the form of that person there. This is our fourth vow. You are bound by the same vow, only with us Sisters, this hunger is more on the material side, and for you Brothers it is spiritual hunger, spiritual nakedness, spiritual homelessness. Believe me, Brothers, I find it much more difficult to work with people who have bitterness, who have anxiety in their hearts, who are unwanted, unloved, uncared-for.

7 The essential must be the same, the same spirit of total surrender, the same satiating of the thirst of Jesus, the same proclamation, the same presence, the same poverty, the same chastity. The four vows must not be different. What you are doing, that love for Christ, that presence and that word of God, we are putting into action. It is the same thing. You are to be his presence with the word, and we are putting his presence into action.

8 This is what we have to learn right from the beginning, to listen to the voice of God in our heart, and then in the silence of the heart God speaks. Then from the fullness of our hearts, our mouth will have to speak. That is the connection. That is a Universal Brother of the Word. In the silence of the heart, God speaks and you have to listen. Then in the fullness of your heart, because it is full of God, full of love, full of compassion, full of faith, your mouth will speak. That's a true Brother of the Word.

Listen in silence, because if your heart is full of other things you cannot hear the voice of God. But when you have listened to the voice of God in the stillness of your heart, then your heart is filled with God, like our Lady full of grace. And then from the fullness of the heart the mouth will speak.

9 You may be writing, and the fullness of your heart will come to your hand also. Your heart may speak through writing. Your heart may speak through your eyes also. You know that when you look at people they must be able to see God in your eyes. If you get distracted and worldly then they will not be able to see God like that. The fullness of our heart is expressed in our eyes, in our touch, in what we write, in what we say, in the way we walk, the way we receive, the way we need. That is the fullness of our heart expressing itself in many different ways. And this is what a Universal Brother of the Word has to live, to understand.

10 It's not enough just to go and become a brotherhood. That's not enough. But it's very important for us to allow Jesus to live his life of love, of prayer, of oneness with the Father. God speaks in the silence of the heart, and we listen. And then we speak to God from the fullness of our heart, and God listens. And this listening and this speaking is what prayer is meant to be: that oneness with God, that oneness with Jesus.

11 As a contemplative, your mouth must be very pure to be able to utter those words of God all the time, just as our hands in our active life must be very pure when we touch the body of Christ. This is something that must be the very life of our life. Otherwise we could rattle off many things, and learn many things by heart, and know all possible knowledge, and all of theology and all the things about God, but we would not be able to light that fire in the hearts of the people. We are just uttering words, not living those words. That is why it is necessary for us that our words be the fruit of our life, the fruit of our prayers, the fruit of our penance, and the fruit of our adoration.

12 There is a very important theologian, a very holy priest, who is also one of the best in India right now. I know him very well, and I said to him, "Father, you talk all day about God. How close you must be to God! You are talking all the time about God." And you know what he said to me? He said, "I may be talking much about God, but I may be talking very little to God." And then he explained, "I may be rattling so many words and maybe saying many good things, but deep down I have not got the time to listen. Because in the silence of the heart, God speaks."

13 It is very important that right from the beginning, Brothers, we simply live the gospel. Live the gospel in prayer; live the gospel in words. Don't be discouraged if you don't reach the height right away. There is no reason for us to be either upset or discouraged, but just one thing is important. That one thing may be nothing in comparison to what people outside expect from you, and yet if you do not put that little drop of prayer, of penance, in your life and in your heart, then the people will be defrauded. You won't be able to give what you don't have.

14 The fullness of our heart comes in our actions: how I treat that leper, how I treat that dying person, how I treat the homeless. Sometimes it is more difficult to work with the street people than with the people in our homes for the dying because the dying are peaceful and waiting; they are ready to go to God. You can touch the sick and believe, or you can touch the leper and believe, that it is the body of Christ you are touching, but it is much more difficult when these people are drunk or shouting to think that this is Jesus in that distressing disguise. How clean and loving our hands must be to be able to bring that compassion to them!

15 You in the West have the spiritually poorest of the poor much more than you have physically poor people. Very often among the rich there are very, very spiritually poor people. I find it is not difficult to give a plate of rice to a hungry person, to furnish a bed to a person who has no bed, but to console or to remove that bitterness, to remove that anger, to remove that loneliness takes a long time.

16 Jesus has made himself the bread of life to satisfy my hunger for him, and he has also made himself the hungry one so that I may satisfy his love for me. He is hungry for us just as we are hungry for him. Universal Brothers of the Word, find out that the Word has to become flesh first in your life, coming among you in love, in unity, in peace, in joy, and then you will be able to give it to the spiritually poorest, to give it to that man sitting in the park, drunk and all by himself.

17 You are Brothers of the Word to be that word. You have been chosen in a special way to enter Nazareth. He has put you here to do just that, to believe in the Word of his Father; that word has life, so you will be able to give that life, Jesus, to all you meet, beginning with your own community, for love begins at home. How does it begin at home? By praying together; a family that prays together stays together.

18 You are to be a family, to be that presence of Christ to each other. Love each other tenderly as Jesus loves each one of you. That is the holiness of the Universal Brothers of the Word: tender love for each other speaks much louder than all the words you can say. Love until it hurts; it takes deep sacrifice to proclaim the word of God. Never hurt anybody with the Word, which is so sacred in our lives. Really live what you say: the younger Brothers that come up learn by seeing, not so much by hearing. Now young people don't want to listen, they want to see.

19 You Brothers who in a special way have taken the word of God, how clean your heart must be to be able to speak from the fullness of your heart! But before you speak, it is necessary for you to listen, for God speaks in the silence of the heart. You have to listen, and only then, from the fullness of your heart, you speak and God listens.

20 What you contemplative Brothers have to bring is your presence, and by that presence you will bring light. Christ must be the light that shines through you, and the people looking at you must see only Jesus. Don't try to be anything else but that. You have a challenge from Jesus to meet: he has shed the light, and you will take his light and lighten every heart you meet. You will not work in big groups or with big numbers, but in the street, in the hospitals, in the jails: any place where darkness has surrounded that person, you are to be the light-bearer.

21 There is a great humility in God. He can stoop down to people like us and become dependent on us for these things to live, to grow, to bear fruit. And he could easily have done it without us. Yet he stooped down and took each of us here to call us together to make this brotherhood. And if you had refused, he couldn't have done it. We could have said no. Each of us could have said no. God would have waited patiently for somebody who would say yes. This is what makes me realize that when Jesus said, "Learn of me for I am meek and humble of heart," he really meant that we should learn that the call is a gift from God himself.

22 The perfect will of God for us: you must be holy. Holiness is the greatest gift that God can give us because for that reason he created us. For that reason you have become Universal Brothers of the Word. You have not come here just to spend time, even to spend your time praying. You have come here to be his love, his compassion. You have been sent.

23 The aim of God, for us to exist, for you, for me, is to be contemplative. It is to be useful to the people by speaking the word of God, by bringing the love of the word of God to the people. How pure, how clean your heart must be, because from the fullness of the heart you have to speak.

24 What is contemplation? To live the life of Jesus. This is what I understand—to love Jesus, to live his life in us, to live our life in his life. That's contemplation. We must have a clean heart to be able to see: no jealousy, anger, contention, and especially no uncharitableness. To me, contemplation is not to be shut up in a dark place, but to allow Jesus to live his Passion, his love, his humility in us, praying with us, being with us, sanctifying through us.

25 Love—really be a contemplative in the heart of the world. Whatever you do, even if you help somebody cross the road, you do it to Jesus. Even giving somebody a glass of water, you do it to Jesus. Such simple little teaching, but it is more and more important.

26 Brothers, to give the word of God, to be the word of God to your people, is the reason for your existence. But you cannot give, you cannot utter that word unless you live that word, unless you pray that word. To be able to give, you must have. To that end you will stay holy, that you may understand what Jesus wants—to be through you and in you.

27 The world today is hungry not only for bread but hungry for love; hungry to be wanted, to be loved. They're hungry to feel that presence of Christ. In many countries, people have everything except that presence, that understanding. That's why the life of prayer and sacrifice comes to give that love. By being contemplative, you are to be that presence, that bread of God to break.

28 People are hungry for the word of God that will give peace, that will give unity, that will give joy. But you cannot give what you don't have. That's why it is necessary to deepen your life of prayer. Allow Jesus to take you, pray with you and through you, and then you will be a real, true contemplative in the heart of the world.

29 We are called to love the world. And God loved the world so much that he gave Jesus. Today he loves the world so much that he gives you and gives me to be his love, his compassion, and that presence, that life of prayer, of sacrifice, of surrender to God. And especially, Brothers, the response that God asks of you is to be a contemplative. Actually, every single Christian, every Catholic who lives a life united in the Eucharist, united with Jesus—he is the contemplative, she is the contemplative.

30 We have a contemplative house in the South Bronx. A taxi driver refused to take me there. The Sisters did not know I was coming, so I had to take a taxi—but he refused to go there. I said, "But we are living there; our young Sisters are living there." He said no. I said, "All right, I will sit near you and you will see that nothing will happen to either you or me." So I got in the taxi and we went. His mouth was open when he saw the young Sisters jumping and laughing, and the people bowing, those who recognized me speaking to me (they were drunk), taking off their hats, and so on. He couldn't get over it, seeing that presence. This is something very beautiful.

31 I remember the first time the contemplative Sisters went into a New York park, they were dressed in white and they prayed the Rosary. When one man saw them he said, "Oh, I'm not ready, I'm not ready." Then the Sisters went a little closer to him and said, "We are Sisters. Jesus loves you." He said, "I am not ready. You have come all the way from heaven, you are angels from heaven to take me. I am not ready." He thought that the angels had come to take him! That shows you what people expect of us.

Eighth Month

1 His love for us led Christ to Gethsemane and to Calvary. Sin did it, our sin and the sins of the world. Sin still does it. If we were all as pure as angels and as honest as saints there could be no need for the Missionaries of Charity (M.C.). God is not being loved and honored as he should by the race he has elevated to the sublime dignity of adopted sons. There is a gap, and God is looking for someone to stand in the gap before him on behalf of this race and beg that he may not destroy it. It is to fill in this gap that we Missionaries of Charity rejoice in what we naturally hate. We do all that we can do just to make God forget the ingratitude of man in return for his boundless love and to make him remember his mercies. He hangs before us on the cross crying out, "I thirst." It is to quench the thirst of this divine Lord that the Missionaries of Charity do all that seems madness to the world. We are truly blessed in having a little share in the following of the cross.

2 See the compassion of Christ towards Judas, the man who received so much love, and yet betrayed his own Master, the Master who kept the sacred silence and would not betray him to his companions. Jesus could have easily spoken in public and told the hidden intentions and deeds of Judas to the others, but he did not do so. He rather showed mercy and charity; instead of condemning him, he called him a friend. If Judas had only looked into the eyes of Jesus as Peter did, today Judas would have been the friend of God's mercy. Jesus always had compassion.

3   Jesus is the Light
                   Jesus is the Truth
                   Jesus is the Life
We too must be:
                   the Light of Charity
                   the Truth of Humility
                   the Life of Sanctity

4 Our works of love are nothing but works of peace. Let us do them with greater love and efficiency, each one in her own or his own work in daily life; in your home, in your neighborhood, it is always the same Christ who says:

I was hungry: not only for food but for peace that comes from a pure heart.

I was thirsty: not for water but for peace that satiates the passionate thirst of passion for war.

I was naked: not for clothes, but for that beautiful dignity of men and women for their bodies.

I was homeless: not for a shelter made of bricks but for a heart that understands, that covers, that loves.

5 For love to be true, it has to hurt. God loved the world so much that he gave his Son. His Son loved the world so much that he gave his life.

And Jesus says: "As the Father has loved me (by giving me to the world), I have loved you (by giving my life for you). Love as I have loved you (by giving yourself)." This giving is prayer, the sacrifice of chastity, poverty, obedience, and whole-hearted free service.

6 We have to love until it hurts. It is not enough to say, "I love." We must put that love into a living action. And how do we do that? Give until it hurts. Some time ago, in our children's home, we didn't have sugar for our children. A little boy, four years old, heard "Mother Teresa has no sugar for the children." He went home and told his parents, "I will not eat sugar for three days. I will give my sugar to Mother Teresa." After three days the parents brought him to our house. He was so small that he could scarcely pronounce even my name, and yet he taught me how to love with great love. It was not how much he gave, but that he gave with great love, and he gave until it hurt.

7 A few weeks ago I got a letter from a little child from the United States. She was making her first Holy Communion. She told her parents, "Don't worry about special clothes for my First Communion. I will make my First Communion in my school uniform. Don't have any party for me. But please give me the money. I want to send it to Mother Teresa." And yet that little one, just seven or eight years old, already in her heart was loving until it hurt.

8 "Whatsoever you did to the least of my brethren, you did it to me." "This is my commandment, that you love one another." Suppress this commandment and the whole grand work of the church of Christ falls in ruins. For Jesus came to earth to give charity its rightful place in the hearts of men. "By this," he said, "men shall know that you are my disciples, if you have love for one another"—and this commandment will last for all eternity. True love for our neighbor is to wish him well and to do good to him.

9 Hear Jesus your co-worker speak to you: "I want you to be my fire of love amongst the poor, the sick, the dying, and the little children; the poor I want you to bring to me." Learn this sentence by heart and when you are wanting in generosity, repeat it. We can refuse Christ just as we refuse others: "I will not give you my hands to work with, my feet to walk with, my mind to study with, my heart to love with. You knock at the door, but I will not give you the key of my heart." This is what he feels so bitterly: not being able to live his life in a soul.

10 A few weeks ago, I picked up a child from the street, and from the face I could see that little child was hungry. I don't know, I couldn't make out how many days that little one had not eaten. So I gave her a piece of bread, and the little one took the bread and, crumb by crumb, started eating it. I said to her, "Eat, eat the bread. You are hungry." And the little one looked at me and said, "I am afraid. When the bread is finished, I will be hungry again." The pain of hunger is something terrible. This little one has already experienced the pain of hunger, which maybe you have never experienced and will never experience. But remember, remember to share the joy of loving by giving until it hurts.

11 If a boy leaves his father's field and goes to work on another, he is no longer his father's co-worker. To be a co-worker means to work along with someone, to share together in tiredness, humiliations, and shame, not only in success. Those who share everything are partners giving love for love, suffering for suffering. Jesus, you have died; you have given everything, life, blood, all. Now it is my turn. I put everything into the field also. The common soldier fights in the ordinary lines, but the devoted one tries to be near the captain to share his fate. This is the only truth, the only thing that matters, for it is the spirit of Christ.

12 We must work in great faith, steadily, efficiently, and above all with great love and cheerfulness; for without this our work will be only the work of slaves serving a hard master.

13 The greatness of our vocation lies also in the fact that we are called upon to minister to Christ himself in the distressing disguise of the poor and suffering. We are called upon every day to exercise our priestly ministry of handling the body of Christ in the form of a suffering humanity and of giving Holy

Communion to all those with whom we come in contact by spreading the fragrance of his love wherever we go.

14 The true interior life makes the active life burn forth and consume everything. It makes us find Jesus in the dark holes of the slums, in the most pitiful miseries of the poor, as the God-Man naked on the cross, mournful, despised by all, the man of suffering, crushed like a worm by the scourging and the crucifixion. It makes us serve Jesus in the poor.

15 I wish to live in this world which is so far from God, which has turned so much from the light of Jesus, to help them—our poor—to take upon me something of their sufferings. For only by being one with them can we redeem them, that is, by bringing God into their lives and bringing them to God.

16 I know you all love the poor—otherwise you would not join—but let each one of us try to make this love more kind, more charitable, more cheerful. Let our eyes see more clearly in deep faith the face of Christ in the face of the poor.

17 Charity for the poor is like a living flame. The drier the fuel, the brighter it burns; that is, our hearts must be separated from earthly motives and completely united to the will of God. Then we shall give free service according to obedience.

18 Keep the love for the poorest of the poor always living. Do not think it is a waste of time to feed the hungry, to visit and take care of the sick and dying, to open and receive the unwanted and homeless. No, this is our love of Christ in action. The humbler the work, the greater should be your love and efficiency. Be not afraid of the life of sacrifice that comes from the life of poverty.

19 We all long for heaven where God is, but we have it in our power to be in heaven with him right now, to be happy with him this moment. But being happy with him now means loving as he loves, helping as he helps, giving as he gives, serving as he serves, rescuing as he rescues—and being with him twenty-four hours a day.

20 My dear children, without our suffering, our work would just be social work, very good and helpful, but not the work of Jesus Christ, not part of the redemption. Jesus wanted to help us by sharing our life, our loneliness, our agony, and our death. All that he has taken on himself, and has carried it into the darkest night; only by being one with us has he redeemed us. We are allowed to do the same; all the desolation of the poor people, not only their material poverty but also their spiritual destitution, must be redeemed and we must share in it.

21 Christ had to deal with the chattering, elbowing crowds, and their very enthusiasm was demonstrative, annoying. They had little thought for his convenience. In their familiarity at times they used to forget him. Yet he would bear with them, let them be as offensive as they might be; always to the end he would have compassion on them. He was not ashamed of sinful men; he would not pass them by, and if they wished it, they could have him as much as anyone else, cost what it might to himself. "I have come," he said, "Not to call the just but sinners to repentance." We Missionaries of Charity are blessed indeed in being called to imitate this tremendous lover of the poor and lonely. Just as Christ, we have to deal with big crowds. We are called to be his co-workers in the slums by letting him radiate and live his life in us and through us in the slums.

22 Let each one of us see Jesus Christ in the person of the poor. The more repugnant the work or the persons, the greater also must be our faith, love, and cheerful devotion ministering to our Lord in this distressing disguise.

23 The more united we are to God, the greater will be our love and readiness to serve the poor wholeheartedly. Much depends on this union of hearts. The love of God the Father for the Son, and of the Son for the Father, produces God the Holy Spirit. So also the love of God for us and our love for God should produce this whole-hearted free service for the poor.

24 Jesus says, "Whatever you do to the least of your brothers is in my name. When you receive a little child you receive me. If in my name you give a glass of water, you give it to me." And to make sure that we understand what he is talking about, he says that at the hour of death we are going to be judged only that way. I was hungry, you gave me to eat. I was naked, you clothed me. I was homeless, you took me in. Hunger is not only for bread; hunger is for love. Nakedness is not only for a piece of clothing; nakedness is lack of human dignity, and also that beautiful virtue of purity, and lack of that respect for each other. Homelessness is not only being without a home made of bricks; homelessness is also being rejected, unwanted, unloved.

25 Pope Paul says that vocation means the capacity to heed the imploring voices of the world of innocent souls of those who suffer, who have no comfort, no guidance, no love.

This requirement is beautifully fulfilled by our vow of whole-hearted and free service to the poor. Just as Christ went about doing good, healing the sick, casting out devils, preaching the kingdom of God, we too spend ourselves untiringly in seeking, in towns as well as villages, even amid the dustbins, the poor, the abandoned, the sick, the infirm, the dying, and in taking care of them, helping them, visiting them, and giving them the message of Christ, and trying our best to bring them to God.

26 We do not accept poverty because we are forced to be poor but because we choose to be poor for the love of Jesus; because he, being rich, became poor for love of us. Let us not deceive ourselves.

27 By the vow of poverty we deprive ourselves of the possession and free use of temporal goods. Its virtue causes the destruction of inordinate attachment to the things of this world. The vow is the means and the virtue is the end. The principal means of observing the essentials of poverty is the strict observance of the common life; that is, everyone, including the superior, should be satisfied with the food, clothing, and outfit given to all alike without the least privilege for any expense but what is truly necessary.

28 We must do our utmost to keep our sight clear and free from the world so that our service to the poor may become one generous act of love. It is this "seeing" that made Fr. Damien the apostle of the lepers, that made St. Vincent de Paul the father of the poor, that made each one of us give up all to serve the poor.

29 To the world it seems foolish that we delight in poor food, that we relish rough and insipid bulgur; possess only three sets of habits made of coarse cloth or old soutanes, mend and patch them, take great care of them and refuse to have extra; enjoy walking in any shape and color of shoes; bathe with just a bucket of water in small bathing rooms; sweat and perspire but refuse to have a fan; go hungry and thirsty but refuse to eat in the houses of the people; refuse to have radios or gramophones which could be relaxing to the racked nerves after the whole day's hard toil; walk distances in the rain and hot summer sun, or go cycling, travel by second-class tram, or third-class overcrowded trains; sleep on hard beds, giving up soft and thick mattresses which would be soothing to the aching bodies after the whole day's hard work; kneel on the rough and thin carpets in the chapel, giving up soft and thick ones; delight in lying in the common wards in the hospital among the poor of Christ when we could easily have private cabins; work like coolies at home and outside when we could easily employ servants and do only the light jobs; relish cleaning the toilets and dirt in the Nirmal Hriday and Shishu Bhavan as though that was the most beautiful job in the world and call it all a tribute to God. To them we are wasting our precious life and burying our talents. Yes, our lives are utterly wasted if we use only the light of reason. Our life has no meaning unless we look at Christ in his poverty.

30 Our Lord gives us a living example: "Foxes have holes and birds of the air their nests and resting places, but the Son of Man has nowhere to lay his head." From the very first day of his human existence he was brought up in a poverty which no human being will ever be able to experience, because "being rich he made himself poor." As I am his co-worker, his "alter Christus," I must be brought up and nourished by that poverty which our Lord asks of me.

31 Our Savior's poverty is greater even than that of the poorest of the world's beasts. "The foxes have holes and birds of the air their nests but the Son of Man has nowhere to lay his head." So it was in fact. He had no house of his own, no fixed abode. The Samaritans had just turned him away and he must seek for shelter. Everything was uncertain: lodging and food. He received whatever he used as alms from the charity of others. Such is indeed great poverty—how touching it is when we think who he is, the God-Man, the Lord of heaven and earth, and what he might have possessed! But it is this which makes his poverty majestic and rich, that it is a voluntary poverty chosen out of love for us and with the intention of enriching us. We are blessed in being called to share in our own little way the great poverty of this great God. We are thrilled also at the magnificent vagabondage of our life. We do not roam, but we cultivate the vagabond spirit of abandonment. We have nothing to live on, yet we live splendidly; nothing to walk on, yet we walk fearlessly; nothing to lean on, but yet we lean on God confidently; for we are his own and he is our provident Father.

Ninth Month

1 There is so much suffering everywhere. Be holy and fervent. God will use you to relieve this suffering. To prove that Christ was divine, that he was the expected Messiah, the gospel was preached to the poor. The proof that this work is God's work is that the gospel is preached to the poor. Pray and thank God for having chosen you to live this life and do this work.

2 Vocation today means also to understand the hard but stupendous mission of the church, now more than ever engaged in teaching man his true nature, his end, his fate, and in revealing to the faithful the immense riches of the charity of Christ.

3 By following the vocation of a Missionary of Charity, we stand before the world as ambassadors of peace by preaching the message of love in action that crosses all barriers of nationality, creed, or country.

The Indian ambassador in Rome told the people, "These our sisters have done more in a short time to bring our two countries closer to each other by their influence of love than we have through official means."

4 We have been instrumental in preaching the word of God to the poor, the neglected, the sorrowful, the lonely of all nations. Unworthy though we are, God has used us to make him known and loved by this God-oblivious world. We have the privilege of entering the very homes of the poor and neglected faithful and thus to pull them and their children out of their beds and bring them together to praise God in the midst of his church, to take part in her sacrifice, and to eat the Lord's Supper. What Vatican II has been asking today, we have by the grace of God been already doing since the very moment of the foundation of our Society.

5 Let us renew our love for the poor. We will be able to do so only if we are faithful to the poverty we have vowed, that we have chosen.

6 As the poor keep growing in poverty due to the great rise in the cost of living, let us be more careful regarding the poverty in our houses. We have the daily needs that our poor cannot get; let us be more careful in the use of them, so that we also feel the hardship in food, clothing, water, electricity, and soap—things which our poor often go without. Because we can get these things easily, we use them in abundance, maybe more than we would use if we were at home.

7 Our clothing should be respectable in order not to displease secular persons and repel them from our service. Yet our clothing must not be handsome nor made from fine material. For reasons of health or due to climate we may have to increase the number of garments, but we should have nothing superfluous. However, we must beware not to mistake want of cleanliness, tidiness, or neatness for poverty. Dirty, un-cared-for clothes are a sign of laziness and riches. They help neither health nor edification. St. Bernard used to say: "I love poverty, not dirt."

8 The sisters should not be ashamed to beg from door to door if necessary, becoming beggars for the poor members of Christ, who himself lived on alms during his public life and whom they serve in the sick and poor.

9 We depend solely on divine providence. We don't accept government grants. We don't accept church donations, we don't accept salaries; we have conse-crated our lives to give the poorest of the poor whole-hearted, free service and the joy of being loved. Our people are longing to be loved. And we have got the tenderness, the love of God that continually dares.

10 When our Lord wanted Sisters for his work among the poor he expressly asked for the poverty of the cross. Our Lord on the cross possessed nothing. He was on the cross, which was given by Pilate. The nails and the crown were given by the soldiers. He was naked when he died; cross, nails, and crown were taken away from him and he was wrapped in a shroud given by a kind heart and buried in a tomb which was not his. Yet Jesus need not have done all this. He could have died as a king and he could have risen from the dead as a king. He chose poverty because he knew in his infinite knowledge and wisdom that it is the real means of possessing God, of conquering his heart, of bringing his love down to this earth.

11 Once the longing for money comes, the longing also comes for what money can give: superfluities, nice rooms, luxuries at table, more clothes, fans and so on. Our needs will increase, for one thing brings another, and the result will be endless dissatisfaction. This is how it comes. If you ever happen to have to get things, remember that the superiors have to depend on you. As a religious you must buy things of cheaper quality and your good example in saving will keep up the spirit of poverty.

12 When at home, the Sisters must keep themselves very busy—working on the farm or making things for sale—for our Lord worked for his mother. He was a real laborer. He was known as the son of the carpenter; he lived a life of hard labor for nearly twenty years, never hesitating, never doubting the will of God, though he came to bring souls to God. In the hard work of his foster father's shop he showed the greatest virtues that a human being can have: humility, obedience, poverty. Always keeping himself above material preoccupations, he—the master of everything—worked not for the work itself but for him who sent him, for his Father in heaven. That is why the pictures of St. Joseph are among the most beautiful we know.

13 As we are and mean to remain poor with the poor for the love of Christ, we willingly offer up the pleasure of our own room. The common dormitory is a means of practicing many virtues: poverty, modesty, cleanliness, and tidiness. It also helps to foster the family spirit.

14 "Whether you eat or sleep do it all for the glory of God." Christ certainly did not feast sumptuously during his life. His parents were poor, and the poor do not feast on the good things of the table. In fact he often endured real want, as the multiplication of the loaves and fishes and the plucking of the ears of grain on walks through the fields teach us. The thought of these instances should be salutary reminders when in the mission or at home our meals are meager. If dishes taste good, thank God; if not, thank him still and thank him even more because he has given you an opportunity to imitate our Savior in his poverty. It would be a defect to speak about food or to complain about what is served; to be occupied with such thoughts at any time is disedifying.

15 A rich man of Delhi, in speaking of our Society, said, "How wonderful it is to see Sisters so free from the world—in the twentieth century when one thinks everything is old-fashioned but the present day." Keep to the simple ways of poverty: of repairing your shoes, and so on—of loving poverty as you love your mother.

16 Don't search for Jesus in far lands—he is not there. He is close to you; he is with you. Just keep the lamp burning and you will always see him. Keep on filling the lamp with all these little drops of love, and you will see how sweet is the Lord you love.

17 I think I'm not afraid for you Brothers if you deepen your personal love for Christ. Then you will be all right. Then people may pass you by, but you will not be hurt, you will not be harmed. The first time you go out they may throw stones at you, all right. Turn the other side—let them throw at the other side also; what is important is that you are holding on, that you have got a grip on Christ and he will not let your hand go.

18 Jesus is going to do great things with you Brothers if you let him do it and if you don't try to interfere with him. We interfere with God's plans when we push in someone or something else not suitable for us. Be very strict with yourself, and then be very strict with what you are receiving from outside. People may come with wonderful ideas, with beautiful things, but anything that takes you away from the reality of what you have given to God must remain outside.

19 Be faithful in little things, for in them our strength lies. To the good God nothing is little, because he is so great and we so small. That is why he stoops down and takes the trouble to make those little things for us—to give us a chance to prove our love for him. Because he makes them, they are very great. He cannot make anything small; they are infinite. Yes, my dear children, be faithful in little practices of love, in little fidelities to the Rule, which will build in you the life of holiness and make you Christlike.

20 My prayer for all families is that you grow in holiness through this love for each other. Bring Jesus wherever you go. Let them look up and see only Jesus in you. Pray for your children and pray that your daughters and sons will have the courage to say yes to God and to consecrate their lives totally to him. There are many, many families that would be so happy if their children would give their lives to God. So pray for them that they will be able to fulfill the heart's desire.

21 By the vow of chastity we give up our hearts to our Lord, to the crucified Christ; the one place in our hearts belongs to him.

In the Gospels, we read that God is like a jealous lover. We cannot have two masters, for we will serve one and hate the other.

The vows themselves are but means of leading the soul to God, and the vow of chastity in particular is intended as a means of giving the heart to God. The heart is one of the highest and noblest of the faculties, but it is also a source of danger. By our vow we consecrate our heart to God and renounce the joys of family life. Yes, we do renounce the natural gift of God to women to become mothers for the greater gift, that of virgins of Christ, of becoming mothers of souls.

22 Our Lord has a very special love for the chaste. His own mother, St. Joseph, and St. John the beloved disciple all were consecrated to chastity. Why do I desire to be chaste? I want to be chaste because I am the spouse of Jesus Christ, the Son of the living God. I want to be chaste because of the work I have to do as the co-worker of Christ. My chastity must be so pure as to draw the most impure to the Sacred Heart of Jesus.

23 We must be convinced that nothing adorns a human soul with greater splendor than the virtue of chastity and nothing defiles a human soul more than the opposite vice. Yet there must be no mistake that the glory of chastity is not in immunity from temptation but in victory over these temptations.

24 Some interior and exterior helps to chastity:
—Diffidence in ourselves and a very special confidence in God and the Sacred Heart of Jesus, who is the fountain and source of all sanctity.

—The memory of the presence of God and the spirit of prayer.

—Frequent reception of the Holy Eucharist which is the wheat of the elect.

—Mortification of the flesh.

—Faithful observances of the rules of modesty and the rule of touch, and supreme contempt for particular friendship. True friendship is a gift of God. Real friendship is affectionate and reserved, is not exclusive, and allows freedom in the choice of friends.

—The spirit of work, even in the hot season.

—Straightforwardness with our superior and with our spiritual father in our confessions.

—Great prudence, especially in dealing with the other sex. Imprudence has caused the ruin of many religious.

—A personal love of our Lady, the virgin undefiled. She will watch over us and if we fail, let us remember that she is the refuge of sinners.

25 When we recollect that in the morning we have held within our hands an all-holy God, we are more ready to abstain from whatever could soil their purity. Hence deep reverence for our own person; reverence for others, treating all with accepted marks of courtesy, but abstaining from sentimental feelings or ill-ordered affections.

26 We must have love, kindness, and heroism that will touch the heart of God and so bring many a soul to the wounded heart of Christ. How pure our hands must be if we have to touch Christ's body as the priest touches him in the appearance of bread at the altar! With what love and devotion and faith he lifts the Sacred Host: the same we too must have when we lift the body of the sick poor. Let us put the same love, faith, and devotion into our action and he will take it as done to him personally.

27 If we love God with our whole soul, if we have a love of Jesus Christ above all things, if we have a tender love for our Lady, we shall be less inclined to be unduly attached to creatures. In order that the love for Jesus may produce these effects, it must be intense, generous, and all-absorbing. It will so fill the mind and heart that we no longer give a thought to human affections. Should we unfortunately become entangled in any ill-ordered affections, Jesus who cannot suffer strange gods in our hearts will reproach us severely. He will himself protect with jealous care the hearts of those who give themselves to him.

28 Today, more than ever, we need to pray for the light to know the will of God, for the love to accept the will of God, for the way to do the will of God.

29 This doing of the will of God is obedience. Jesus came to do the will of his Father and did it unto death, death on the cross. "Be it done to me according to your word," was our Lady's answer for you and for me when we have been chosen to be his own by becoming Missionaries of Charity. The surest way to true holiness and the fulfillment of our mission of peace, love, and joy is through obedience.

30 Fidelity in the least things, not for their own sake—for this is the work of small minds— but for the sake of the great thing, which is the will of God and which I respect greatly in little things. St. Augustine says: "Little things are indeed little, but to be faithful in little things is a great thing." Is not our Lord equally present in a small Host as in a great one? The smallest rule contains the will of God as much as the big things of life.

Tenth Month

1 As our Society keeps growing, naturally there is a danger of that beautiful spirit of family diminishing. It is for each one of us to protect it and make the life of love and unity, of humility and service, live and bring much fruit in each one of us and in the people we serve. In order to protect this family spirit of love and unity in spiritual life, we must be able to uplift each other and through the good example of a life of prayer and union with God, encourage and help each other to remain faithful to our vocation.

2 Truly He has loved me unto death. Do I love Jesus unto death? How can I love Jesus whom I do not see if I don't love my Sister or Brother—or the poor—whom I do see? If I do not, St. John says: "You are a liar."

3 The beautiful name, "sister," is another strong tie of the members of the same family. The sacredness of it is so great that King Solomon, in his Song of Songs, calls the soul by this sweet name.

4 In the poor, and in our Sisters and Brothers, it is Jesus, and so we are twenty-four hours in his presence. Therefore we are contemplatives in the heart of the world. If we would only learn how to pray the work by doing it with Jesus, for Jesus, to Jesus, for the glory of his name and the good of souls!

5 If sometimes we feel as if the Master is away, is it not because I have kept myself far from some Sister? One thing that will always secure heaven for us: acts of charity and kindness with which we have filled our lives. We will never know how much good just a simple smile can do. We tell people how kind, forgiving, and understanding God is—are we the living proof? Can they really see this kindness, this forgiveness, this understanding, alive in us?

6 Holiness grows so fast where there is kindness. I have never heard of kind souls going astray. The world is lost for want of sweetness and kindness. In religious houses this kindness is in greater danger, for we have grown so much used to each other that some think they are free to say anything to anybody at any time. They expect the other Sisters to bear with their unkindness. Why not try first to put a brake on your own tongue? You know what you can do, but you do not know how much the other can bear. Why not give the chance of holiness to yourself first? Your holiness will be of greater help to your Sisters than the chance you give her to put up with your unkindness.

7 If you don't have love for one another, then how can you love Christ? How can they see Jesus in you? That's why we need a clean heart, to see Jesus. Love one another. That's all Jesus came to teach us. The whole gospel is very, very simple. Do you love me? Obey my commandments. He's turning and twisting just to get around to one thing: love one another. He wants us to be really, really loving. Give from the heart.

8 Be kind in your actions. Do not think that you are the only one who can do the efficient work, work worth showing. This makes you harsh in your judgment of the other Sisters who may not have the same talents. God will ask of that Sister only what he has given her, and not what he has given you; so why interfere with the plan of God? All things are his, and he gives as he pleases. You do your best and think that others do their best for God's own purpose. Their best may be a total failure—what is that to you? You follow the way he has chosen for you. For others also, let him choose.

9 Intense love does not measure; it just gives. To be an apostle of the Sacred Heart, one must be burning with love, intense love for the Sisters. If you want peace, you cannot just say anything you please, the first word that comes into your head.

10 Thoughtfulness is the beginning of great sanctity. If you learn this art of being thoughtful, you will become more and more Christlike, for his heart was meek and he always thought of others. Jesus "went about doing good." Our Lady did nothing else in Cana, but thought of the need of the others and made their need known to Jesus. The thoughtfulness of Jesus and Mary and Joseph was so great that it made Nazareth the abode of God Most High. If we also have that kind of thoughtfulness for each other, our communities will really become the abode of God Most High.

11 How beautiful our convents will become where there is this total thoughtfulness of each other's needs! The quickest and the surest way is the tongue: use it for the good of others. If you think well of others, you will also speak well of others and to others. From the abundance of the heart the mouth speaks. If your heart is full of love, you will speak of love.

12 Let us be very sincere in our dealings with each other and have the courage to accept each other as we are. Do not be surprised or become preoccupied at each other's failure; rather see and find in each other the good, for each one of us is created in the image of God. Jesus has said it so beautifully: "I am the vine, you are the branches." Let us try to see and accept that every Sister is a branch in Christ the vine. The same life-giving sap that flows from the vine through each of the branches is the same.

13 In one word, be a real branch on the vine, Jesus. The surest means to this will be to deepen our love for each other: knowing each other's lovableness; feeling the need of each other; speaking well of each other and to each other; appreciating and knowing each other's gifts and abilities.

14 "If a man loves me, he will keep my word."
"My new commandment: Love one another as
I have loved you."

"My Father will love him and we will come to him
and make our home with him."

In loving one another through our works we bring
an increase of grace and a growth in divine love. Since
Jesus' love is our mutual love we will be able to love as
he loves, and he will manifest himself through us to
each other and to the world; by this mutual love they
will know that we are his.

15 These words of Jesus, "Love one another, even
as I have loved you," should be not only a light
to us, but they should also be a flame consuming the
selfishness which prevents the growth of holiness.
Jesus "loved us to the end," to the very limit of love:
the cross. This love must come from within, from our
union with Christ. It must be an outpouring of our
love for God, superior and Sisters in one family, a
family with the common Father, who is in heaven.
Loving must be as normal to us as living and
breathing, day after day until our death.

16 Love begins at home, right inside our community. We cannot love outside unless we really love our Brothers and Sisters inside. So I say we
need a very clean heart to be able to see God. When
we all see God in each other, we will love one another
as he loves us all. That is the fulfillment of the law, to
love one another. This is all Jesus came to teach us: that
God loves us, and that he wants us to love one another
as he loves us.

17 St. Therese the Little Flower said: "When I act and think with charity, I feel it is Jesus who works within me. The closer I am united with him, the more I love all the other dwellers in Carmel." To understand this and practice it we need much prayer, which unites us with God and overflows continually upon others. Our works of charity are nothing but the overflow of our love for God from within. Therefore the one who is most united to him loves her neighbor most.

18 How beautiful it is to see the love for each other a living reality! Young Sisters, have deep love and respect for your older Sisters. Older Sisters, treat your younger Sisters with respect and love, for they, like you, belong to Jesus. He has chosen each one of you for himself, to be his love and his light in the world. The simplest way of becoming his light is by being kind and loving, thoughtful, and sincere with each other: "By this they will know that you are his disciples."

19 Let us understand the tenderness of God's love. For he speaks in the Scripture, "Even if a mother could forget her child, I will not forget you. I have carved you on the palm of my hand." When you feel lonely, when you feel unwanted, when you feel sick and forgotten, remember you are precious to him. He loves you. And show that love for one another, for this is all that Jesus came to teach us.

20 Let us ask our Lady and St. Joseph to make our communities what they made Nazareth for Jesus. Let us not be afraid. Jesus said, "Be not afraid, I am with you" and "Love one another as I have loved you"—by this they will know that you belong to Jesus. Love does not live on words, nor can it be explained by words—above all that love which serves him and comes from him and which finds him, touches him, serves him, loves him in others. Such love is true, burning, pure, without fear and doubt— no greater love than the love Christ himself has shown us. So I ask you to love one another as he has loved us. As the Father has loved him, he has loved us, and loves us now. He has called us by our name; we are precious to him.

21 Individuals of any nationality are welcome in our Society because in this as in everything else we want to be true children of our holy Mother Church. Nationalism is inconsistent with our constitutions, and renders us unfaithful to the spirit of our vocation. Hence we should never fasten an unfavorable opinion on people belonging to another nation than ours, for this would speak great want of charity.

22 St. Clement related having heard from St. Peter that our Lord was accustomed to watch like a mother with her children, near his disciples during their sleep to render them any little service.

Such is the chain that unites and binds us, the old with the young, a chain of gold, a thousand times stronger than flesh and blood, interest or friendship, because these permit the defects of the body and the vices of the soul to be seen, while charity covers all, hides all, to offer exclusively to admiration and love the work of the hands of God, the price of the blood of Jesus Christ, and the masterpiece of the Holy Spirit.

23 We must not be afraid to proclaim Christ's love and to love as he loved. In the work we have to do—it does not matter how small and humble it may be—make it Christ's love in action. Do not be afraid to keep a clean and undivided heart and to radiate the joy of being the spouse of Christ crucified. Do not be afraid to go down with Christ and be subject to those who have authority from above and who therefore declare Christ's obedience unto death. Rejoice that one more Christ is walking through the world in you and through you going about doing good.

24 The most important rule of a well-regulated family, of a family founded on love and unity, is that the children show an unbounded trust in and obedience to their parents. Jesus practiced this for thirty years in Nazareth, for we hear nothing of him but that "he was subject to them," that is, he did what he was told.

25 Our obedience, by being prompt, simple, blind, and cheerful, is the proof of our faith. If God loves a cheerful giver, how much more would he not love a "cheerful obeyer"? We must obey as Christ obeyed—unto death, even death on the cross. He saw the will of his Father in everything and everybody, so that he could say, "I do the things that are pleasing to him." He obeyed Caiaphas and Pilate because their authority was given "from above." He submitted to them with obedience and dignity. He did not look at the human limitations of Caiaphas and Pilate. He looked at his Father, for whose love he submitted himself to them. Let us obey like Jesus and our lives would become pleasing to God and he would say, "This is my beloved child in whom I am well pleased."

26 Obedience well lived frees us from selfishness and pride and so it helps us to find God and in him the whole world. Obedience is a special grace and it produces unfailing peace, inward joy, and close union with God.

27 Obedience transforms small, commonplace things and occupations into acts of living faith, and faith in action is love, and love in action is service of the loving God. Obedience lived with joy creates a living awareness of the presence of God, so that fidelity to acts of obedience such as the bell, timetable, or the eating of food, that are the fruit of constant, prompt, cheerful, undivided obedience, become like drops of oil that keep the light of Jesus living in our life.

28 If we really want to grow in holiness through obedience let us turn constantly to our Lady to teach us how to obey, to Jesus who was obedient unto death: he, being God, "went down and was subject to them."

29 This complete surrender of self to God must secure for us perseverance in God's service, since by obedience we always do his most holy will and consequently obtain freedom from doubts, anxieties, and scruples.

30 We are infallible when we obey. Ask the Holy Spirit to give us that one grace. Only Jesus in the Blessed Sacrament, Jesus on the cross, can teach us obedience, and that is by the reality of his own example.

31 A certain priest loved the Chinese and wanted to do something for them. He became so involved in the work that it seemed that even his eyes became slanted, like the Chinese. If I live constantly in the company of Jesus, I will look like him and do as he did. Nothing pleases God more than when we obey. Let us love God not for what he gives but for what he deigns to take from us. Our little acts of obedience give us the occasion of proving our love for him.

Eleventh Month

1 As Jesus in his Incarnation became one of us in everything except sin, we too when sent as contemplative missionaries to new countries or new states within the same country, in true contemplative missionary spirit shall:

—detach ourselves from our own land, culture and language

—learn to love the new land and its people, learn their language, and be acquainted with their history, culture, and religious beliefs

—respect their customs and ways and yet as members of the International Religious family retain our freedom to use what is sacred, beautiful, and necessary from the cultures of any people and nation in the whole family of God, adopting, however, in a very special way, the culture, customs, and ways of Jesus Christ and his saints which will never be out of fashion and which contain the best in all the cultures of the whole world.

2 If we join the Community outside our own country, or are sent on a mission, we shall freely choose

to be there, happy to suffer and die with the people if need arises, and ready to remain there till obedience calls us back.

In adapting ourselves to the standard of living of the people among whom we are, we shall sacrifice what is not strictly necessary for our life, remembering that we are relating not just to the poor of that country but to the poor of the whole world.

3 Total surrender—for us, contemplative life means also a joyous and ardent response to his call to the most intimate union with him by:

—totally abandoning ourselves into his hands,

—yielding totally to his every movement of love, giving him supreme freedom over us to express his love as he pleases, with no thought of self,

—desiring with ardent desire all the pain and delight involved in that union.

It also means:

—to be a willing prisoner of his love, a willing victim of his wounded love, a living holocaust, and

—even if he cuts us to pieces, to cry out, "Every piece is yours."

4 Loving trust means for our contemplative life:

—an absolute, unconditional, and unwavering confidence in God our loving Father, even when everything seems to be a total failure,

—to look to him alone as our help and protector,

—to stop doubting and being discouraged, casting all our worries and cares on the Lord, and walking in total freedom,

—to be daring and absolutely fearless of any obstacle, knowing that nothing is impossible with God, and

—total reliance on our Heavenly Father with a spontaneous abandonment of the little children, totally convinced of our utter nothingness but trusting to the point of rashness with courageous confidence in his fatherly goodness.

5 Cheerfulness is indeed the fruit of the Holy Spirit and a clear sign of the kingdom within. Jesus shared his joy with his disciples: "that my joy may be in you and that your joy be full" (Jn 15:11). Our joy is a work of our generosity, selflessness, and close union with God; for he gives most who gives with joy, and God loves a cheerful giver.

6 We shall go freely in the name of Jesus, to towns and villages all over the world, even amid squalid and dangerous surroundings, with Mary the Immaculate Mother of Jesus, seeking out the spiritually poorest of the poor with God's own tender affection and proclaiming to them the good news of salvation and hope, singing with them his songs, bringing to them his love, peace, and joy.

7 We shall call sinners to repentance, and turn them to God by our personal concern for them, proclaim to them the mercy of God, and when necessary remind them also of the justice of God, and teach them the way to salvation through abnegation and the cross, through a total change of mind and heart, through belief in the name of Jesus, and through liv-

ing his message of love for the Father and one's neighbor.

8 We shall instruct the ignorant by the power of the example of our lives lived entirely in and with Jesus Christ our Lord, bearing witness to the truth of the gospel by our single-minded devotion to and burning love of Christ and his church, and also by verbal proclamation of the Word of God fearlessly, openly, and clearly, according to the teaching of the church, whenever opportunity offers.

9 We shall counsel the doubtful by listening to them attentively, lovingly, and prayerfully and then speaking to them the truth of God, firmly, gently, and with love.

We shall sustain the tempted by our prayer, penance, and understanding love and when opportunity offers also by enlightening and encouraging words.

We shall befriend the friendless and comfort the sick and sorrowful by our real love and personal concern for them, identifying ourselves with them in their pain and sorrow and by praying with them for God's healing and comfort and by encouraging them to offer their sufferings to the Lord for the salvation of the whole world.

10 We shall bear wrongs patiently by offering no resistance to the wicked—if anyone hits us on the right cheek by turning the left also; if anyone takes away anything from us by not trying to get it back.

We shall forgive injuries by seeking no revenge but returning good for evil, by loving our enemies and praying for those who persecute us and blessing those who curse us.

We shall bring prayer into the lives of the spiritually poorest of the poor by praying with them and for them and making them personally experience the power of prayer and the reality of the promise of Jesus, "Ask and you shall receive. Whatever you ask in my name I will do."

11 Humility is truth; therefore in all sincerity we must be able to look up and say, "I can do all things in him who strengthens me." Because of this assertion of St. Paul, you must have a certain confidence in doing your work—or rather God's work— well, efficiently, even perfectly—with Jesus and for Jesus. Be also convinced that by yourself you can do nothing, that you have nothing, but sin, weakness, and misery: that all the gifts of nature and of grace which you have, you have them from God.

12 The missionary aspect of our call to contemplation will find its expression in going in haste to the spiritually poorest of the poor

—personally, to proclaim the peace, joy, and love of God wherever we are sent, as well as

—in spirit, to every part of the vast creation of God from the furthest planet to the depths of the sea, from one abandoned convent chapel to another abandoned church, from an abortion clinic in one city to a prison cell in another, from the source of a river in one continent to a lonely mountain cave in another, and even into heaven and the gates of hell, praying with and for each of God's creation to save and sanctify each one for whom the blood of the Son of God has been shed.

13 The contemplative aspect of our missionary call makes us gather the whole universe and bring it to the very center of our heart, where he who is the source and the Lord of the universe abides, and remain in communion with him, drinking deeply from the very source the deep calm and peace of interior quietude and refreshment of God, allowing the pure water of divine grace to flow plentifully and unceasingly from the source itself on to the whole of his creation.

14 The universal aspect of our life of contemplation makes us pray and contemplate with all and for all, especially with and for the spiritually poorest of the poor of the whole world.

15 The simplicity aspect of our life of contemplation makes us see the face of God in everything, everyone, everywhere, all the time, and his hand in all the happenings, and makes us do all that we do—whether we think, study, work, speak, eat, or take our rest—in Jesus, with Jesus, for Jesus and to Jesus, under the loving gaze of the Father, being totally available to him in any form he may come to us.

16 We shall not waste our time in looking for extraordinary experiences in our life of contemplation but live by pure faith, ever watchful and ready for his coming by doing our day to day duties with extraordinary love and devotion.

17 Our contemplation is pure joy in our awareness of the presence of the Lord. It is pure silence in our experience of his fullness. Our contemplation is our life. It is not a matter of doing but being. It is the possession of our spirit by the Holy Spirit breathing into us the plentitude of God and sending us forth to the whole creation as his personal message of love.

18 Our life of contemplation is simply
—to realize God's constant presence and his tender love for us in the least little things of life, and
—to be constantly available to him, loving him with our whole heart, whole mind, whole soul, and whole strength, no matter in what form he may come to us.
We are called to remain immersed in the contemplation of the Father, Son, and the Holy Spirit in their love for one another as well as in their love for us manifested in the great marvels of creation, redemption, and sanctification.

19 We shall not rely much on books written by men to learn how to contemplate but place ourselves before Jesus and ask him to send us his Spirit to teach us how to contemplate.

20 Formation will be given not so much by words, but by the living example of those in charge of formation, as well as of each one in the community, and also by prayer, sacrifice, and real personal concern for them preparing the way for the Lord in their lives.

21 Jesus who contemplates in us is also the rock of our contemplation, our forest of meditation, desert of solitude, our hermitage, and cave in whom we enter to remain deep in contemplation of God in communion with all our brothers and sisters.

22 We shall spend two hours a day at sunrise and sunset in adoration of Jesus in the Blessed Sacrament exposed. Our hours of adoration will be special hours of reparation for sins, and intercession for the needs of the whole world, exposing the sin-sick and suffering humanity to the healing, sustaining, and transforming rays of Jesus, radiating from the Eucharist.

23 The contemplatives and ascetics of all ages and religions have sought God in the silence and solitude of the desert, forest, and mountain. Jesus himself spent forty days in the desert and long hours in communing with the Father in the silence of the night on the mountains.

24 We too are called to withdraw at certain intervals into deeper silence and aloneness with God, together as a community as well as personally, to be alone with him, not with our books, thoughts, and memories but completely stripped of everything, to dwell lovingly in his presence: silent, empty, expectant, and motionless.

25 Our penance is an act of perfect love of God, man, and the whole universe. It seeks to reconcile man with God, man with man, and man with

God's creation, bringing about the unity in Jesus, with Jesus, and through Jesus of all that was disrupted by sin. It is for us a joyful identification with Christ crucified; it is a hunger to be lost in Him, so that nothing remains of us but he alone in his radiant glory drawing all men to the father. "Unless a grain of wheat falls on the ground and dies it remains a single grain, but if it dies it yields a rich harvest" (Jn 12:24).

26 Just as the rigorous winter prepares the way for spring, penance prepares us for the sanctity of God, filling us with his vision and love. It makes us more and more sinless and attunes us to the work of the Spirit within us, bringing our whole being under the powerful influence of Jesus. It plunges us into the deep contemplation of God.

27 "We are an exile from the Lord's presence as long as we are at home in the body and still desire the things of this world" (St. Francis of Assisi). No contemplation is possible without ascetism and self-abnegation. "The road to God demands one thing necessary: True self denial, exterior and interior, through surrender of self both to suffering for Christ and to annihilation in all things" (St. John of the Cross).

28 We shall make use of our gestures and postures in prayer to grow in the depth of prayer and contemplation of God by using them meaningfully and with devotion. Therefore, we shall
—use the holy water with devotion as a sign of interior cleansing and blessing of God;

—make the sign of the cross beautifully as a sign of belonging entirely to the Father, Son, and Holy Spirit, set aside totally for contemplation and love, sealed against the powers of the flesh, world, and the devil;

—keep our hands joined in prayer as a sign of deep reverence and adoration of God;

—kneel and genuflect with devotion as a sign of adoration, supplication, intercession, humility, and penance;

—pray standing straight in liturgical prayer as a sign of our community participation of the people of God in the public worship of the church—the pilgrim church on the way to the Father—our liberation and resurrection in Christ, and of our respect, alertness, and readiness for anything;

—pray sitting with deep recollection as a sign of listening, docility, intimacy, contemplation, and loving trust;

—bow low in adoration as a sign of total surrender.

29 We shall do our utmost to introduce and encourage personal and family prayer, meditation and prayerful reading, and if possible sharing the word of God in the Scriptures in every home we visit.

30 We deliberately renounce all desires to see the fruit of our labor, doing all we can as best we can, leaving the rest in the hands of God.

Twelfth Month

1 There are three signs of genuine humility; see if you possess these:

1. Deference, respect, and obedience towards your superiors.

2. The joyous acceptance of all humiliations.

3. Charity towards your Sisters, particularly towards those who are poor and humble.

2 How will I become humble? By humiliations that come to me, by accepting myself as I am, and by rejoicing at infirmity. Naturally we don't like this, but confidence in God can do all things. It is our emptiness and lowliness that God needs and not our plentitude. A fervent Sister is conscious of her own weakness and tries to be happy when others see her weakness.

3 These are the few ways we can practice humility:
To speak as little as possible of oneself.
To mind one's own business.
Not to want to manage other people's affairs.
To avoid curiosity.

To accept contradiction and correction cheerfully.
To pass over the mistakes of others.
To accept insults and injuries.
To accept being slighted, forgotten and disliked.
Not to seek to be specially loved and admired.
To be kind and gentle even under provocation.
Never to stand on one's dignity.
To yield in discussion even though one is right.
To choose always the hardest.

4 Let us not forget that we owe humility to God out of reverence to him, or that our humility is not only an imitation of Christ but also a perfect way of giving oneself to Jesus, for when we are able to accept with joy all these humiliations, our love for Jesus becomes very intimate and very ardent.

5 What is not humility:
Neediness when humiliated, when corrected.
Trying always to excuse oneself.
Refusing to acknowledge one's fault, even dishonestly.
Putting the blame on somebody.
Ambition to acquire praise.
Yearning to be in charge of everything, to control all.

6 If you are humble, nothing will touch you, neither praise nor disgrace, because you know what you are. If you are blamed, you won't be discouraged; if anyone calls you a saint, you won't put yourself on a pedestal. If you are a saint, thank God; if you are a sinner, don't remain one. Christ tells us to aim very

high, not to be like Abraham or David or any of the saints, but to be like our heavenly Father.

7 The season of Advent is like springtime in nature, when everything is renewed and so is fresh and healthy. Advent is also meant to do this to us—to refresh us and make us healthy, to be able to receive Christ in whatever form he may come to us. At Christmas he comes as a little child, so small, so helpless, so much in need of his mother and all that a mother's love can give. It was his mother's humility that helped her to do the works of handmaid to Christ—God from God, true God from true God. Let us see and touch the greatness that fills the depths of their humility. We cannot do better than Jesus and Mary. If we really want God to fill us, we must empty ourselves through humility of all that is selfishness in us.

8 Let us beg from our Lady to make our hearts "meek and humble" as her Son's was. It was from her and in her that the heart of Jesus was formed. Let us all try during this month to practice humility and meekness. We learn humility through accepting humiliations cheerfully. Do not let a chance pass you by. It is so very easy to be proud, harsh, moody, and selfish—so easy. But we have been created for greater things; why stoop down to things that will spoil the beauty of our hearts? How much we can learn from our Lady! She was so humble because she was all for God. She was full of grace. She made use of the almighty power that was in her, the grace of God.

9 Humility always radiates the greatness and glory of God. How wonderful are the ways of God! He used humility, smallness, helplessness, and poverty to prove to the world that he loved the world. Let the Missionaries of Charity not be afraid to be humble, small, and helpless to prove their love to God.

10 It is in loving our Lord and our neighbor that our humility will flower, and it is in being humble that our love will become real, devoted, and ardent.

11 Let us really take the trouble to learn the lesson of holiness from Jesus, whose heart was meek and humble. The first lesson from this heart is our examination of conscience, and the rest—love and service—follow at once. Examination is not our work alone, but a partnership between us and Jesus. We should not waste our time in useless looks at our own miseries, but should lift our hearts to God and let his light enlighten us and make him to have his way with us.

12 God wants us to be close to him. St. John says that he opened his heart. Become small and then you will be able to enter it. It is one thing for me to say I am a sinner, but let someone else say that about me and then I feel it; I am up in arms. If I am falsely accused I may suffer, but deep down there is joy, whereas if the correction be founded on even a small reality—something in me having deserved it—then often it hurts more. We must be happy that our faults are known as they are and be open with the superiors about faults and shortcomings.

13 You may have visions and ecstasies and yet be deceived. Watch! There are the silk threads of pride and deception, for example, hiding good qualities: a good voice, the ability to make others happy, and so on. "I cannot do this. I cannot do that—but I can be lazy." Pride is often covered by laziness.

14 Complaining and excusing oneself are most natural, but they are a means the devil makes use of to increase our pride. Correction at times hurts most when it is most true.

15 Humility is the mother of all virtues: purity, charity, obedience. St. Bernard and all the saints built their lives on humility. Charitableness and pride cannot go together because pride is all for self, and charity wants to give. The sisters most liked are those who are humble. Self-knowledge puts us on our knees, and it is very necessary for love. For knowledge of God gives love, and knowledge of self gives humility.

16 Self-knowledge is very necessary for confession. That is why the saints could say they were wicked criminals. They saw God and then saw themselves—and they saw the difference. Hence they were not surprised when anyone accused them, even falsely. They knew themselves and knew God. We take hurt because we do not know ourselves, and our eyes are not fixed on God alone; so we do not have real knowledge of God. When the saints looked upon themselves with such horror, they really meant it. They were not pretending.

17 We must also be able to make the distinction between self-knowledge and sin. Self-knowledge will help us to rise up, whereas sin and the weakness that leads to repeated sin will lead to despondency. Deep confidence and trust will come through self-knowledge. Then you will turn to Jesus to support you in your weakness, whereas if you think you are strong, you will not need our Lord.

18 Humiliations come also from most unexpected corners, as from the chosen people of God themselves: the bishops, priests, and nuns. We are looked down on by some because of our lack of culture or education, our inefficiency in our work for lack of proper qualifications, or because of our awkwardness. Some do not understand our way of life or our charity to the poor and so they criticize us. Even so Christ was despised by the very cream of his own nation, the chief priests and the Pharisees. So we are blessed again in sharing the same lot as Christ, though in a very small way.

19 Joy is not simply a matter of temperament in the service of God and souls; it is always hard—all the more reason why we should try to acquire it and make it grow in our hearts.

20 Joy is a need and a power for us, even physically. A Sister who has cultivated a spirit of joy feels less tired and is always ready to go doing good. A Sister filled with joy preaches without preaching. A joyful Sister is like the sunshine of God's love, the hope of eternal happiness, the flame of burning love.

21 Joy is one of the best safeguards against temptation. The devil is a carrier of dust and dirt; he uses every chance to throw what he has at us. A joyful heart knows how to protect herself from such dirt. Jesus can take full possession of our soul only if it surrenders itself joyfully. "A saint who is sad is a sad saint," St. Francis de Sales used to say. St. Teresa was worried about her Sisters only when she saw any of them lose their joy.

22 To children and to the poor, to all those who suffer and are lonely, give them always a happy smile; give them not only your care but also your heart.

We may not be able to give much but we can always give the joy that springs from a heart that is in love with God. Joy is very infectious. Therefore, be always full of joy when you go among the poor.

23 Someone once asked me, "Are you married?" And I said, "Yes, and I find it sometimes very difficult to smile at Jesus because he can be very demanding sometimes." This is really something true. And there is where love comes—when it is demanding, and yet we can give it to him with joy.

24 We desire to be able to welcome Jesus at Christmas time, not in a cold manger of our heart but in a heart full of love and humility, in a heart so pure, so immaculate, so warm with love for one another.

25 The coming of Jesus at Bethlehem brought joy to the world and to every human heart. The same Jesus comes again and again in our hearts during Holy Communion. He wants to give the same joy and peace. May his coming this Christmas bring to each one of us that peace and joy that he desires to give. Let us pray much for this grace of peace and joy in our own heart, in our communities, in our Society, and in the church.

26 Jesus came into this world for one purpose. He came to give us the good news that God loves us, that God is love, that he loves you, and he loves me. He wants us to love one another as he loves each one of us. Let us love him. How did the Father love him? He gave him to us. How did Jesus love you and me?—by giving his life. He gave all that he had— his life—for you and me. He died on the cross because he loved us, and he wants us to love one another as he loves each one of us. When we look at the cross, we know how he loved us. When we look at the manger we know how he loves us now, you and me, your family, and everybody's family with a tender love. And God loves us with a tender love. That is all that Jesus came to teach us, the tender love of God. "I have called you by your name, you are mine."

27 Cheerfulness and joy was our Lady's strength. This made her a willing handmaid of God, her Son, for as soon as he came to her she "went in haste." Only joy could have given her the strength to go in haste over the hills of Judea to do the work of handmaid to her cousin. So with us too; we like her must be true handmaids of the Lord and daily after Holy Communion go in haste, over the hills of difficulties we meet in giving whole-hearted service to the poor. Give Jesus to the poor as the handmaid of the Lord.

28 Joy is prayer; joy is strength; joy is love, a net of love by which you can catch souls. God loves a cheerful giver. He gives most who gives with joy. If in the work you have difficulties and you accept them with joy, with a big smile—in this, as in any other good thing—they will see your good works and glorify the Father. The best way to show your gratitude to God and people is to accept everything with joy. A joyful heart is the normal result of a heart burning with love.

29 "Who do you say that I am?" (Mt 16:15). You are God.
You are God from God.
You are begotten not made.
You are one in substance with the Father.
You are the Son of the Living God.
You are the second Person of the Blessed Trinity.
You are One with the Father.
You are in the Father from the beginning;
  All things were made by you and the Father.

You are the beloved Son in whom the Father is well
   pleased.
You are the son of Mary, conceived by the Holy Spirit
   in the womb of Mary.
You were born in Bethlehem.
You were wrapped in swaddling clothes by Mary
   and put in a manger full of straw.
You were kept warm by the breath of the donkey
   who carried your mother with you in her womb.
You are the son of Joseph,
   the carpenter as known by the people of Nazareth.
You are an ordinary man without much learning,
   as judged by the learned people of Israel.

30 Who is Jesus to me?
Jesus is the Word made flesh.
Jesus is the Bread of Life.
Jesus is the Victim offered for our sins on the cross.
Jesus is the sacrifice offered at holy Mass for the sins of
the world and for mine.
Jesus is the word—to be spoken.
Jesus is the truth—to be told.
Jesus is the way—to be walked.
Jesus is the light—to be lit.
Jesus is the life—to be lived.
Jesus is the love—to be loved.
Jesus is the joy—to be shared.
Jesus is the sacrifice—to be offered.
Jesus is the peace—to be given.
Jesus is the Bread of Life—to be eaten.
Jesus is the hungry—to be fed.
Jesus is the thirsty—to be satiated.
Jesus is the naked—to be clothed.

Jesus is the homeless—to be taken in.
Jesus is the sick—to be healed.
Jesus is the lonely—to be loved.
Jesus is the unwanted—to be wanted.
Jesus is the leper—to wash his wounds.
Jesus is the beggar—to give him a smile.
Jesus is the drunkard—to listen to him.
Jesus is the mentally ill—to protect him.
Jesus is the little one—to embrace him.
Jesus is the blind—to lead him.
Jesus is the dumb—to speak for him.
Jesus is the crippled—to walk with him.
Jesus is the drug addict—to befriend him.
Jesus is the prostitute—to remove from danger and befriend her.
Jesus is the prisoner—to be visited.
Jesus is the old—to be served.

31 To me—
Jesus is my God.
Jesus is my spouse.
Jesus is my life.
Jesus is my only love.
Jesus is my all in all.
Jesus is my everything.

JESUS, I love with my whole heart, with my whole being.

I have given him all, even my sins, and he has espoused me to himself in all tenderness and love.

Now and for life I am the spouse of my crucified Spouse.

Amen.

Appendix

Rule of Life and Covenant of the Universal Brothers of the Word

"To Me to Live Is Christ."

"There is a very great need among young people for the Brothers of the Word—contemplatives in the heart of the world—by their life of prayer, adoration, contemplation, penance and total surrender to God and by their presence and the spoken Word of God for two to three hours daily to the poorest of the poor. By so doing they will proclaim Christ to all nations and make the Church fully present in the world of today." (Mother's letter to Pope Paul VI, 12/21/77)

"The more simple the Constitutions are, the more like the gospel they will be. Slowly live the gospel and from that life constitutions will grow." (Mother's letter to the Brothers, 6/10/78)

Association of Christian Faithful Founded by Mother Teresa

1. *Our Call*
Our brotherhood, known as the Universal Brothers of the Word, is an "association

of the Christian faithful" founded by Mother Teresa of Calcutta with life commitments of chastity, poverty, obedience, and wholehearted free service to the spiritually poorest of the poor.

International Character

2. By its international character, our brotherhood partakes of that special mission of the Church: To shed on the whole world the radiance of the gospel message and to unify under one spirit all men of whatever nation, race, or culture, standing forth as a sign of that brotherliness which allows honest dialogue and is invigorated by it.

Community of Brothers in Jesus the Lord

3. We believe that we have been called by the Father in the likeness of the first Christians to be a community of Brothers in Jesus, the Lord; to follow Him through the inspiration, teachings, and example of Mother Teresa of Calcutta; and to be of one heart and mind: in a com-

munity of goods, in humble submission to one another and to the Servant Leader, remaining single for the Lord, daily persevering in prayer, adoration, and the "breaking of the Bread," and also being available as carriers of his Word to the spiritually poorest of the poor in season and out of season to the extremity of the world.

Contemplatives in the Heart of the World

4. Our vocation is to be Universal Brothers, carriers of God's love, contemplatives in the heart of the world, monks and missionaries, committed to bring with our life, the Word to the world in the spirit of ecumenism promoted by Vatican Council II.

Universal Brothers of the Word

5. *Our Name*

To evidence our vocation rooted in the universality of the Catholic Church, we will be called "Universal Brothers of the Word." This means that, for Jesus' sake, we want to be Brothers to each and every human being, regardless of color, culture, or creed and for that purpose we want to remain humble, little, and vulnerable, to love until it hurts.

The Word is the eternal "Logos" of the Father, who became the incarnate Word in Mary, who lived in the flesh, who died for our salvation, and he is our risen Lord Jesus Christ, alive and real among us today. Speaking to us and guiding us, we gather in his Name. We covenant ourselves to Him and to each other, to follow in his way, with a joyful and undivided heart by the power of the Holy Spirit.

"I Thirst"

6. *Our aim*
"I will give saints to Mother Church." (Mother)

Our Mission: "To Proclaim Jesus, Saviour to All Nations"

Our aim is to quench the thirsting Jesus on the cross for love of souls and the hunger of souls for Him, the Word and Bread of Life. Our specific mission is to labour for the salvation and sanctification of the spiritually poorest of the poor all over the world, wherever they may be, by:

Knowing the word of God through daily meditation, study, and sharing of Scriptures;

Living the Word of God in prayer and action in a life marked by the simplicity of the gospel;

Loving the Word of God Incarnated: under the appearance of Bread, to satisfy mankind's hunger through our daily adoration and Spirit-filled celebration of the Holy Eucharist;

Speaking the Word of God to the spiritually poorest of the poor in whose distress Jesus is disguised so that they may be restored to the lost image and relationship with the Father. This apostolate of prayer, contemplation, and service shall be our specific vocation: that Jesus Christ be proclaimed "Saviour" to all nations.

Total Surrender, Loving Trust, and Cheerfulness

7. *Our Spirit*

"Our ideal is no one but Jesus." (Mother)

Our spirit is one of total surrender to God, loving trust in each other, and cheerfulness to everyone as was lived by the Holy Family in Nazareth. "Make your family another Nazareth where Jesus can come and rest awhile" (Mother's letter the Brothers, June 7, 1979). Jesus Christ was entirely at the disposal of his Father for the ransom of many. "Though he was God, he did not count equality with God a thing to be grasped, but emptied himself taking the form of a servant, being born in the likeness of men" (Phil 2:5-8).

Total Surrender

8. To be possessed by him so that we may possess him, to take whatever he gives and to give whatever he takes with a big smile; to be used by him as it pleases him without being consulted; to offer him our free will, our reason, our

whole life in pure faith, so that he may think his thoughts in our minds, do his work through our hands, and love with our hearts.

Our total surrender consists also in being totally available to God and his Church through our availability to our Servant Leader, our Brothers, and the peoples we serve. It is thus we will be all powerful with him who strengthens.us.

Loving Trust　9. Jesus trusted his Father with an unshakable trust. His trust was the fruit of his intimate knowledge and love of the Father. He trusted his Father so completely that he entrusted his whole life and the mission for which he was sent into the hands of his Father. He was fully confident that his Father would work out his plan of salvation in spite of the ineffectual means used and the apparent failure.

Cheerfulness　10. Joy is indeed the fruit of the Holy Spirit and a characteristic mark of the kingdom of God, for God is joy. Christ wanted to share his joy with his apostles, "That my joy may be in you and that your joy may be full" (Jn 15:11). Our joy is a sign of our generosity, selflessness, and close and continual union with God. A joyful heart is the normal result of a heart burning with love, for he gives most who gives with joy, and God loves a cheerful giver.

A Brother filled with joy preaches without preaching. Joy is a need and a power for us even physically, for it makes us always ready to go about doing good.

Therefore we shall accept: to live the life of poverty in cheerful trust, to offer cheerful obedience from inward joy, to minister to Christ in his distressing disguise with cheerful devotion. This cheerfulness will be the best way to show our gratitude to God and to people.

Reborn in Christ

11. *Means*

Reborn in Christ by water

and the Spirit and established in the Church as a community of life in faith, hope, and charity, we who enter into the mysteries of Christ's life ought to be molded into his image "until He is formed in us" (Gal 4:19).

Faith

12. Faith, a gift of God, introduces us into the spiritual reality of the Kingdom, whose coming was announced by Christ. It grows in obedience to his law and expresses itself by fraternal charity. Finally it is sealed by fidelity and confidence "for we know in whom we have placed our faith" (2 Tm 1:12). It is he who grants to those that believe in him, to do greater things even than those he himself did on earth.

With an interior conviction, we live and do things which we would never have dreamed of doing. As Universal Brothers of the Word, we are especially called upon to see Christ in the appearance of bread and to touch him in the brokenness of the spiritually poorest.

Hope

13. In hope we rely utterly on the omnipotence of him who said: "Without me you can do nothing." Persuaded of our nothingness and with the blessing of obedience, we attempt all things, doubting nothing, for with God all things are possible. We will allow the good Lord to make plans for the future, for yesterday has gone, tomorrow has not yet come, and we have only *today* to make Him known, loved, and served. Grateful for the thousands of opportunities Jesus gives us to bring hope into a multitude of lives by our concern for the individual sufferer, we will help our troubled world at the brink of despair, to discover a new reason to live or to die with a smile of contentment on its lips.

Charity

14. God is love: Charity has its source in the eternal love of the Father and the Son in the Spirit. We allow the Spirit of love to take possession of

us, to break all barriers to love, to make us open to others at the very depths of our being, capable of receiving both God and mankind.

Christ when he took bread said: "Take and eat, this is my Body delivered for you." By giving himself, he invites us to grow in the power of his love to do what he has done. Christ's love for us will give us strength and urge us to spend ourselves for him. "Let the Brothers and the people eat you up." We have no right to refuse our lives to others in whom we contact Christ.

Meek and Humble of Heart

15. Jesus, anxious that we learn from him that one lesson to be meek and humble of heart, allowed his heart to be opened. We must become small to be able to enter his heart. Christ, our way to humility, asks us to live in him and by him. Convinced that by ourselves we can do nothing and have nothing but sin, weakness, and misery, we acknowledge all gifts of nature

and of grace as gifts of God. We do not allow ourselves to be disheartened by any failure as long as we have done our best; neither do we glory in our success but refer all to God in deepest thankfulness. We will meditate frequently on the humility of Christ and pray to the Holy Spirit for light, to know ourselves better, since self-knowledge leads to humility. God does not ask us to be successful but faithful.

Following Christ: Life of Prayer and Contemplation

"Shoulder my yoke and learn from me, for I am gentle and humble of heart, and you will find rest for your souls. Yes, my yoke is easy and my burden light" (Mt 11:29-30, JB).

Evangelical Counsels

16. *Gospelship*

We have a contemplative-oriented religious life that is rooted in the Evangelical Counsels and marked by the simplicity, joy, and freedom of the gospel, and keeping with the best traditions of the Church in her Eastern and Western expressions, fully open to all that is beautiful and sacred in the cultural and spiritual heritage of the people among whom we live and serve.

Metanoia by the Power of the Spirit

17. Upon entering the Brotherhood, we will stive with all our might to seek that "metanoia," or "conversion of heart," to be born again with power in newness of life and become simple and sincere like little children.

For that purpose we will foster a vital devotion to the Holy Spirit, preparing ourselves for the Feast of Pentecost with an eight-day yearly retreat.

Continual Prayer

18. Mindful of the precept of the Lord that we should pray always, all our life should be gradually transformed into a life of prayer, adoration, and communion with the indwelling Presence of the Holy Trinity so that whatever we may do at all, we do it for the glory of God, always praying our work but never

substituting our prayer with work.

The Breaking of the Bread

19. The breaking of the Bread in the Lord's Supper will always be the eventful center of our daily life, source of our apostolate, alive with the Spirit and full of holy joy.

Adoration

20. We will have two hours daily of adoration, usually at the rising and the setting of the sun, and every Saturday night, in preparation for the Lord's Day, we will have a vigil of intercessory adoration in the middle of the night.

Holy Scripture

21. "The Church has always venerated the divine Scriptures just as she venerates the Body of the Lord, since from the table of both the Word of God and the Body of Christ she unceasingly receives and offers to the faithful the Bread of Life, especially in the sacred liturgy. She has always regarded the Scripture, together with sacred tradition, as the supreme rule of

faith, and will ever do so" (VC II, Dog. Const. on Div. Rev., C. 6, art. 21). The Word of God in Scripture is our rule of life, our way of living. We share in it as an individual and as a community every day. We go to it for light, for wisdom, for direction, for correction and healing, growing in the knowledge that "man does not live by bread alone but by every word that comes from the mouth of God" (Mt 4:4, JB).

Veneration of the Bible

22. The Bible will be solemnly enthroned in our chapels, and it will be the object of particular veneration.

Divine Office

23. In our life of prayer, great freedom and openness to the promptings of the Spirit, spontaneity, and creativity will be encouraged. Hence, it should not be rigidly structured but remain flexible and free. The morning, noon, evening, and night will normally form our daily community prayer, which can be recited or chanted. We also

can make use of posture and gesture, yet appropriately and with discretion.

Liturgical Seasons

24. A keen sense of the liturgical seasons and their meaning should be developed in the prayer life of the community in order to be guided and nourished within and without by the proper spirit of the liturgical year.

Spiritual Reading

25. A period of spiritual reading, *Lectio Divina,* will complement the daily adoration of the Blessed Sacrament. One hour will be devoted to the reading of the Word of God in the Holy Scripture, yet we can also make use of commentaries of the Fathers of the Church and well-known spiritual authors of both Eastern and Western traditions.

Sacrament of Reconciliation

26. Jesus, Son of God, became Word made flesh and accepted suffering and death freely for man's redemption from sin. He calls us: "Take up your cross and follow me"

(Mt 16:24) and "unless you repent you will all likewise perish" (Lk 13:3).

The call to penance is a call to conversion: from sin to God, from mediocrity to a life of fervor and generosity, from fervor and generosity to a life of sanctity. No contemplation is possible without asceticism and self-abnegation.

The Sacrament of Penance is Christ's Easter gift of joy and peace for our salvation and sanctification. We shall receive it not only for our own reconciliation with God and with one another, but also for the whole of sinful humanity.

We should value frequent confession. Our Servant Leader will secure for us the possibility of confession at least every two weeks, though we are free to approach it more often, according to our need and choice.

We will do our utmost to help our poor to love confession and to feel the need of it.

Revision of Life

27. The Servant Leader, periodically and at a suitable time, should call the community to a "revision of life," where the Brothers in the light of the Scripture and in a spirit of great charity will examine their conduct and fraternally correct each others' faults.

Reparation and Mortification

28. Sharing the Passion of Christ relived in the suffering poor—in a spirit of reparation for our sins and the sins of the world, especially the ones of selfishness, injustice, greed, and waste—we shall fast on bread and water every Friday of the year with the exception of the times of Christmas, Easter, and major feasts when they fall on Friday.

Brothers of the Word in Silence

29. *Brothers of Silence*
"So I will allure her; I will lead her into the desert and speak to her heart" (Hosea 2:16 NAB).
"Souls of prayer are souls of great silence" (Mother).

To be true Brothers of the Word, we must in the first place be true brothers of silence. God is the friend of silence; his language is: "Be still and know that I am God." He requires us to be silent to discover him. In the silence of the heart God speaks, since silence is the language of the contemplative and solitude is his dwelling.

Silence: Source of Communication

30. In the Eucharist, Jesus' silence is the highest and the truest proclamation of the praise of the Father; hence, we have to put silence at the root of our union with him and with one another. Without it our whole life as Universal Brothers of the Word will collapse, for:
the fruit of silence is prayer,
the fruit of prayer is faith,
the fruit of faith is love and
the fruit of love is service.

Times and Places of Silence

31. Out of genuine love for one another, we shall provide for each other in the house an at-

mosphere of peace and quiet, facilitating prayer, study, work, and rest. For this purpose we will have particular times and places where a greater silence and solitude will be possible. In so doing we will cultivate a deeper spirit of recollection and become more aware and awake to that ever indwelling presence of God in our heart, the hearts of others, and in every minute detail of his whole creation.

Special Periods of "Desert" or Poustinia

32. Our silence is joyful and God-centered silence; it demands of us constant self-denial and plunges us into the depths where intimacy and oneness with the Lord become reality.

Like Jesus, who spent forty days in the desert communicating with the Father, we too are called to withdraw at certain intervals into deeper silence and aloneness with God, together as a community as well as individually.

The Servant Leader shall

always keep a few rooms or huts set apart for any Brother sincerely desiring to spend a "desert time" in silence and solitude.

Houses of Prayer

33. Our houses will always remain houses of prayer and reconciliation where the spiritually poorest of the poor, without distinction of creed, color, and nationality, are welcome and can make peace with God.

Associates

34. As part of our apostolate we shall also remain open to receive among us young men who sincerely wish temporarily to live our way of life purely for the love of God and salvation of the poor, without any obligation to stay longer. They must, however, fulfill the conditions necessary to our way of life. They will live in separate quarters under the direction of a Brother assigned to them for that purpose.

Enclosure

35. To be able to be alone with God and with our Brothers

in an atmosphere of silence and peace, every house shall have a part reserved for the exclusive use of the Brothers. No other persons shall be admitted into it, save such persons that are exempt according to the law of the Church.

The enclosure will comprise at least the dormitory, the refectory, and the rooms where the Brothers are usually working and studying.

Hermitages

36. As far as possible, our houses of prayer will be in an open place, conducive to silence and contemplation. They will not be too far from the poor. If possible, a simple little hut or room for each one, allowing greater silence, solitude, and intimacy with God, should be provided. If this is not possible, the Brothers shall be content with the lack of privacy and space, happy to share in the lot of the poor.

Signs of Belonging to Jesus

37. *Uniform*
As a sign of our belonging to Jesus and having entered a

new state of life by religious consecration and our desire for effacement, we shall wear a religious uniform: a simple shirt with a crucifix pinned over the heart, pants, and sandals.

For the Eucharistic Liturgy and other important occasions, the Brother can use a white cassock with cincture, prayer shawl, and rosary like the one Mother Teresa gave to the first Brothers of the Word at the beginning of our foundations at San Gregorio al Celio, Roma.

We receive a new religious name at the time of profession. We call each other "Brother," including the priests, if any. We keep our hair short as a sign of renunciation of secular ways. We wear sandals and remain barefooted at home, as far as possible, and are always without shoes in the chapel as a sign of humility, nakedness before the Lord, and also as walking on sacred ground.

Following the example of the Saints, we will make ourselves plain and little in every aspect of life.

Call to the Depths of Silence: Sharing in Jesus' Passion

38. With Jesus our Saviour, "Lamb led to the slaughter," and with the poor, we will accept cheerfully and in a spirit of faith all the opportunities he gives to us of a greater gift: to share in the silence, loneliness, and agony of his passion in our life, due to humiliations, misunderstanding, false blame, rejections, failure, incapacities, corrections, temptations, lack of virtue, separations, sickness, old age, and death.

God spoke one Word and he spoke in eternal silence, and that Word is his Son Incarnate: Jesus Christ. We must hide in the silence of his mystery to be able to know, to love, to live, and to give him.

Our Patroness and Advocate

39. *Mary, First Carrier of the Word*
"So he said to his mother, 'He is your son.' Then he

said to the disciple, 'She is your mother'" (Jn 19:26).

"Mary, first Carrier of God's Word, help the Universal Brothers to become humble like you, so that they can become holy like Jesus" (Mother).

We proclaim Mary, the Mother of Jesus and our Mother, the first Carrier of the Word and Queen of peace in the universe, as special patroness and advocate to our Brotherhood. The Feasts of her Annunciation and Visitation will be our patronal feasts to be prepared and celebrated with special solemnity. On either day of her feast, together we will renew our commitments and our consecration to her.

Devotion to Mary

40. Devotion to Mary is the fruit of the Incarnation of Jesus, Word of God made flesh for us.

Mary was a true Carrier of the Word because:
Though full of grace, she was not afraid to be the handmaid of the Lord.

Like her we will do what she did: empty ourselves, receive Jesus as Word and Bread of Life, and give him in haste to the spiritually poorest of the poor.

Though conceived Immaculate, she met Jesus humiliated, carrying his cross; and near the cross she stands and intercedes for us sinners in need of redemption.

Like her we will accept the cross in whatever way it comes, acknowledging our need of redemption and that of our brothers throughout the world.

The recitation of the Mysteries of the holy Rosary in the street, and as a daily family prayer, is an expression of our tender devotion to Mary and has been a custom of our Brotherhood since the very beginning.

At the School of Our Lady

41. As a Brotherhood we will be learning from Mary at the

school of Nazareth. She who taught Jesus to be meek and humble of heart will teach us to do the same. She who kept God's Word, pondering it in her heart, will teach us silence and prayer. She who at Cana was aware of people's needs will teach us delicate, tender love and service, which is the fruit of obedience.

Perseverance in our vocation and in God's friendship are the supreme graces Our Lady will infallibly obtain for anyone who turns to her. "Be it done to me according to your Word" was Our Lady's answer for each one of us who has been chosen to be his own by becoming Universal Brothers of the Word. And so with Mary, Mother of the Church, we will bring the Word made flesh to dwell in the hearts of all men. Mary, first Carrier of the Word, pray for us.

The address of Mother Teresa is:
Mother Teresa M.C.
54 A Lower Circular Rd.
Calcutta. W. B. 700016 India

The address of the Universal Brothers of the Word is:
334 Northeast 26 Terrace
Miami, Florida 33137 U.S.A.

Also available in Fount Paperbacks

Mother Teresa: Her People and Her Work
DESMOND DOIG

'Desmond Doig has written a beautiful book and his writing and the pictures capture Mother Teresa and her people and her work exactly. He understands it. I want to cry, with anger, with passion, with compassion, with sadness at the waste of human life and energy. But no, that is not enough, it is a waste of energy, we must do something to help her.'

Financial Times

Something Beautiful for God
MALCOLM MUGGERIDGE

'For me, Mother Teresa of Calcutta embodies Christian love in action. Her face shines with the love of Christ on which her whole life is centred. *Something Beautiful for God* is about her and the religious order she has instituted.'

Malcolm Muggeridge

A Gift for God
MOTHER TERESA

'This selection of Mother Teresa's sayings, prayers, meditations, letters and addresses on themes of love and compassion . . . touches profound spiritual themes . . . Its size belies its power to inspire and uplift.'

Church of England Newspaper

The Love of Christ
MOTHER TERESA

A further collection of Mother Teresa's writings and sayings, including hitherto unpublished extracts from her retreat addresses to her community of nuns.

'Do not read this book . . . if you do not want . . . to be shaken in conscience and shamed into loving God and other people more.'

Iain Mackenzie, Church Times